GEORGE W. GARDNER
in The Argonne Forest
France, 1917
Germany, 1918-1919

This book, a loving tribute to George W. Gardner's wartime service, was compiled from stories, articles, documents and photographs gathered from family scrapbooks.

ISBN 1-58597-374-2

Library of Congress Control Number: 2005937132

4500 College Boulevard
Overland Park, KS 66211
888-888-7696
www.leatherspublishing.com

Dedicated to
Rick Martin
and
Ray Martin
by their mother,
Joyce M. Martin

This volume is also dedicated to the
Honor Roll of the 353rd Infantry

—

"And oftimes cometh our wise Lord God, Master of
every trade,
And tells them tales of His daily toil of Edens newly
made,
And they rise to their feet as He passes by, gentlemen
unafraid."

INTRODUCTION

My father, George W. Gardner, the son of Jonas and Maryetta Gardner, was born in a sod house northwest of Traer, Kansas, on November 14, 1888. He attended school three to four months out of the year. He was not able to attend high school, for he had to help support his family financially, which consisted of nine brothers and sisters. His father, whose occupation was farming until the year 1917, believed that when you reached the age of 16 you were able to make your own way in life.

GEORGE W. GARDNER

Address: Oberlin, Ks.

Entered Service: 7 Sept 1917.

Branch of service: U.S. Army Infantry.

Trained at: Camp Funston, Ks. (Sept. 1917 to May 1918).

Overseas: May 1918.

Returned to U.S.: May 1919.

Theatre of Operations: European (France).

Engagements: St. Mihiel; Argonne Forest.

Decorations: Distinguished Service Cross; Croix De Guerre.

Discharged: 1 June 1919 at Camp Funston, Ks.

Rank: Sergeant.

Total time served: Twenty-one months.

Occupation: Farming, until death, 1965.

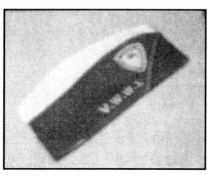

Let's turn back to the year 1917 relating to George W. Gardner, Army No. 2176371. He entered service on September 7, 1917, his number being the first called out of Decatur County. Refer to opposite page. Also included: "Traer Shows Patriotism" and the "Thank You" to all who were included.

TRAER SHOWS PATRIOTISM

George Gardner, the third son of J.R. Gardner, of Traer, was one of the first men called under the draft. He was called to report at Fort Riley, Saturday of last week, and his people gave him a farewell party Wednesday evening when more than 150 people attended and were served with ice cream and cake.

He was escorted to Oberlin Friday by about everybody in Traer. There were twelve autos all loaded to capacity. Father Walton, the only old soldier left at Traer, took the lead and carried a large American flag. This car was followed by others loaded with George's relatives and friends.

George Gardner is one of the good boys of the county, and he is deserving of this demonstration of the love and esteem in which he is held by those knowing him best. He left Oberlin Friday evening on the Burlington.-Booster

October 21st.
Oberlin HERALD, OBERLIN, Kans.

We are all feeling good and getting plenty of drill. There are quite a lot of the boys leaving. About 4000 from the Depot Brigade and I expect it will catch all of the boys who came down here after we did. They will be sent to various camps throughout the U.S. to fill up the regular army and national guard, but I think the 353rd Regiment will be in Camp Funston all winter, at least until the first of the year. The first 5 percent that came down from Decatur county are all in the 353d and all are holding down non-commissioned offices with a good chance to make good. Almost all the 353d barracks have steam heat, and those that have not will probably have some this coming week. The weather has been fine down here, very few days but what the sun shone, but I expect that there will be plenty of storms later to make up for it. Will close for this time.

— Geo. W. Gardner

CARD OF THANKS

I am taking this manner of expressing my thanks to the Royal Neighbors for the lunch and various things they sent me, which were greatly appreciated.

Geo. W. Gardner

UNITED STATES SOLDIERS fought bravely in World War I. "The war to end all wars," but since the day the Armistice was signed on Nov. 11, 1918, thousands of United States military units have gone to battle in World War II, the Korean and Vietnam Wars and Desert Storm.

The Oberlin Herald carried news of hometown boys in its columns throughout all the battles of the Great War, often with personal letters from servicemen.

The United States declared war on Germany on April 6, 1917. *The Herald* reported on Sept. 13, 1917:

THE FIRST TO GO

On Friday evening, the first installment of the men called to the colors came to Oberlin and in the evening left for Fort Riley. They were **George W. Gardner,** Glenn Wookey, Frank W. Tacha, Leo Bendon. A goodly number of people were in the city to see the boys off. The McKay Martial Band was present, the school children sang "America," and then led by the band, the boys fell in and marched to the depot. The boys were all in finest spirits and will no doubt give a good account of themselves when they get to the front.

On May 2, 1918, a patriotic gathering in Oberlin was recorded in *The Herald:*

On Friday afternoon at 4 p.m., there gathered several hundred people in front of the courthouse and listened to the songs of the high school and addresses that were inclined to make a man feel glad that he was an American. O.L. Benson, in behalf of the Treasury Department of the U.S., presented to the city of Oberlin the Third Liberty Loan honor flag, given for having oversubscribed the city's quota in the drive.

The Herald recorded on May 30, 1918, a farewell was given for servicemen who left together.

"… I have no pity for the dead,
    They have gone out, gone out with flame and song,
A sudden shining glory round them spread;
    Their drooping hands raised up again and strong;
Only I sorrow that a man must die
To find the unending beauty of the sky."

THE LIFE OF A SOLDIER

By Opal Hamper, Age 12, 7th grade.

In the year of 1917 there was such a demand for soldiers that every man in the United States between the age of 21 and 31 was called upon to register June the fifth. These men were then under the draft law. On September seventh the same county boys were called to camps, my uncle, George Gardner, being one of them.

When the day arrived for him to leave home, a crowd of his friends from Traer, in automobiles decorated in flags and bunting, accompanied him to Oberlin where he was to appear before the local board and meet the other three boys who were to leave from there with him. The music was furnished by the military band, while the boys marched to the depot. They disappeared from our view in the passenger coach and were on their way to camp.

On the morning of September 8th they arrived at Camp Funston in time to eat their first meal.

The first few days the boys were issued their uniforms and clothing and put into companies composed of 250 men in which he was put into Company A, 353 Infantry. During this time he took his vaccinations. Then after a few weeks he was transferred into Company F, into the same regiment.

The soldiers' beds are single cots, each soldier sleeping alone.

When the meals are ready, each soldier is supplied with a mess kit knife, fork and spoon and march through the kitchen, where their eats are all put on the mess kit, then march on to a long table, where they have benches for chairs. There they sit down and eat.

When the companies go out on the field to drill, each officer has a certain number of men under his charge. My uncle is a sergeant. They are drilled in small bunches at first. After a while they were issued rifles and sent out on the rifle range to practice shooting, marching at all times to and from their work.

My Uncle George was kept training in camp until May 25, 1918, when the 89th division started for New York. When the train arrived at Lake Erie, it stopped. The soldier boys all got off and took a bath in the Lake. My Uncle George picked up a small clam shell on the shore and sent it home to grandma. Several towns between Camp and New York they were treated very nice by the Red Cross, serving hot coffee and eats of some kind.

While in New York he was made platoon sergeant.

At 11 o'clock on the morning of June 3rd the 89th division set sail across the ocean. After a tiresome voyage of several days they landed in England. They were then sent to France.

In a short time they were then sent to the front and kept there until the armistice was signed.

In a battle November 2nd he was rewarded with a gold medal for his bravery, leading his battalion thru shell and machine gun fire, capturing two machine guns and destroying several others.

After the armistice was signed, the 89th division was transferred into the Army of Occupation to follow the Germans back to the River Rhine. The Americans started this march back November 16th, 1918.

ENLISTMENT RECORD.

Name: _George W Gardner_   Grade: _Sergeant_

Enlisted, or Inducted: _Sept 7_, 191_7_ at _Oberlin Kas_

Serving in _____ First _____ enlistment period at date of discharge.

Prior service : * _none_

Noncommissioned officer: _Sergeant Oct 18, 15_

Marksmanship, gunner qualification or rating : T _Marksman_ _____

Horsemanship: _Not mounted_

Battles, engagements, skirmishes, expeditions _Lucy Sector Tome Sltte to Sept 12, 1918_ _____ _St Mihiel Offensive Sep 12 to 16, 1918 — Lucey Sector France Sept 17 to Oct 7 - Meuse Argonne_ _____ _Field War France Chevron_

Knowledge of any vocation: _Farmer_

Wounds received in service: _none_

Physical condition when discharged: _Good_

Typhoid prophylaxis completed _March 11, 1919_

Paratyphoid prophylaxis completed _March 11, 1919_

Married or single: _Single_

Character: _Excellent_

Remarks: _____ _absent from duty under GO #5_ _14 of 31-19. entitled to reduced railroad fare and_ _travel pay to Oberlin Kans_ _served in Co F 353rd Infantry_

Signature of soldier: _George W Gardner_

_____

Commanding _F 353rd Inf_

TRANSPORTATION ISSUED.

LIST OF PERSONS CALLED INTO THE SERVICE OF THE UNITED STATES NOT EXEMPTED OR DISCHARGED

Form No. 146, prepared by the Provost Marshal General Local Board for Decatur County, State of Kansas, Oberlin, Kansas.

District Board: Local Board for Decatur County, State of Kansas, Oberlin, Kansas, hereby certifies to District Board for the Second District, State of Kansas, Wichita, Kansas, the following list of the names and addresses of persons who have been duly and legally called for the military service of the United States, and who have not been exempted or discharged.

Certified to District Board August 13th, 1917.

258 George W. Gardner, Traer 1
564 Robert S. Diehl, Oberlin 8
548 Clyde M. McKay, Dresden .. 11
437 Earl E. Miller, Norcatur 24
 43 Glen B. Wookey, Kanona 26
625 Roy B. Rees, Jennings 28
797 John W. Seigenthaler, Oberlin 32
432 William Steveris, Norcatur .. 34
....
 75 Byron E. Babb, Kanona 47
721 Fred S. Preston, Oberlin 49
280 Charles F. Warrick, Clayton . 51
332 James Dowd, Oberlin 53
379 Jesse L. Conley, Jennings 54
343 Russell G. Conley, Jennings 60
355 Leo Bendon, Jennings.......... 64
530 William Knitig, Selden 65
218 Melvin D. Cook, Dresden 67
56 Edward W. Hatch, Kanona ... 78
549 John C. McKay, Dresden 83
440 Andrew L. Bell, Norcatur 84
711 Horace P. Reasoner, Oberlin 86
353 Carl W. Lieber, Jennings 95
571 George J. Guenther, Oberlin 98
 72 Thomas C. Park, Kanona ... 101
356 Jacob W. Smith, Jennings... 102
679 Wincle Shaffer, Oberlin 105
363 William H. Foster, Jennings . 95
327 Albert Miller, Oberlin 109
 93 Edwin R. Peterson, Oberlin 111
 51 Henry W. Heilman, Jennings 116
 30 Roy P. Spohrer, Clayton 116
199 Michael J. Karla, Dresden.. 119
406 Carl O. Friedeman, Oberlin 123
576 Carl H. Schultz, Oberlin 130
122 Anthony Janousek, Kanona 131
297 Harry P. Witham, Norcatur 135
736 Frederick M. Arehart, Oberlin 137
121 Fred Janousek, Kanona 143
292 John A. Shick, Norcatur..... 145
504 Glenn W. Tice, Dresden 146
191 Charles T. Hoppas, Dresden 150
477 Franklin W. Logan, Oberlin 151
753 Thomas T. Counter, Oberlin 152
657 Elmer D. Ufford, Oberlin ... 156
175 Roy C. Bainter, Dresden 157
300 Ora L. Tilton, Norcatur 158
532 Ture A. Marcuson, Dresden 161
212 Florian M. Wagner,
      Belleview, IA 163
305 Thomas J. Moore, Norcatur 166
323 Roy Dyer, Oberlin 171
539 Newell W. Schuler, Selden . 181
349 Frank W. Tacha, Jennings... 182
 86 James M. Corcoran, Oberlin 187

HOW MEN WILL GO TO CAMPS

WASHINGTON, Aug. 9 — Regulations under which the new national army will be called to the colors, beginning September 1, were issued tonight by Provost Marshal General Crowder. They detail the program under which every soldier of the draft army has been accepted by the adjutant general of the training cantonment to which he is assigned.

The actual call for men will go from the provost marshal general to the state adjutant general. Each local board will be informed of its proportion and the adjutant general will fix the date when men from his state shall entrain for camps.

The local board will make out the list of men to fill the call from the roll of accepted men and will fix the place and time of entrainment.

From the time specified for reporting to the local board for military duty, each man in respect of whom notice to report has been posted or mailed shall be in the military service of the United States.

Prior to the arrival of the men at board headquarters, board members are instructed to find clean and sanitary lodging, houses and to arrange for meals. In its discretion, the boards may grant permission for the men to remain at their homes.

Arrived at the board headquarters at the hour fixed for reporting, the men will be drawn up, the roll called and agents will take them personally to their quarters, remaining with them until every arrangement for their comfort has been made. Instructions are given that the quality of food furnished shall be good, and the board is held liable for seeing that meals are adequate.

Retreat roll call at board headquarters, set for 5:30 o'clock the afternoon of the day of reporting to the board, will be the first military ceremony the drafted men pass through. The board members are directed to be present in person and to inform the men of their military status, impressing on them the fact that disobedience of order is the gravest military crime. The light hand baggage containing toilet articles and a change of underclothing, which the men are permitted to take with them to camp, will be inspected by the board and the list of men sent forward made out and copies of original registration cards prepared.

For each district five alternates will be summoned to board headquarters in addition to men selected to fill the board quota. They will be held at the assembling point until train time to fill in vacancies should any of the levy fail to report.

Except for retreat roll call, the men will be given town liberty until 45 minutes before train time. The board will select one man from the levy to place in charge of the party for its trip, and he will name a second in command. The other men will be told that orders of these two men must be obeyed under pain of military discipline.

Final verification of the list will be made just before entraining, and if anyone is missing, an alternate will be sent in his place.

It will be the duty of the commander of each party to watch over his men on the trip, see that none is left behind at any station, that all are fed regularly and that no liquor is furnished. Should a train be delayed by accident, the commander of each party will telegraph the camp adjutant general for instructions.

After the departure of the levy for camp, the local board will gather up straggles. If there is evidence of willful violation of orders, the offender will be reported to the adjutant general of the army as a deserter, and the local police will be asked to arrest him on sight and turn him over to the nearest army post for trial. Where there was no intention to desert and the missing man reports of his own will, the board will send him on to the camp with an explanation and a recommendation as to his capability.

Arrived at the camp, the party will undergo final physical examination by army doctors. If any are rejected, the local board will be notified and an alternate sent forward for each such case. — *Kansas City Star.*

ROSTER

Society of the 353rd Infantry

JOHN C. HUGHES, SECRETARY,
829 East Ave. B, Hutchinson, Kansas

ARIZONA
CASA GRANDA
Loebel, W.G., Box 533 (Hdq)
DEWEY
Allen, Hugh, Cherry Route (F)
MESA
Christian, H.M., RFD 2, Box 256, Apache Trail (F)
MIAMI
Cox, Archie C., 918 Keegan St. (F)
PHOENIX
Benson, Earl, 721 E. Coronado Road (K)
Gill, Lew W., 125-1/2 N. 1st Ave. (H)

ARKANSAS
CENTERTOWN
John, Reynolds, H. (Sup)
FAYETTEVILLE
Bradley, O.Z., 108 E. Maple (Hdq)
LITTLE ROCK
Alexander, D.B., 421 Brown (C)
MOUNTAIN HOME
Adamson, Max (K)
Taylor, Alfred (Sup)
RUSSELLVILLE
Hyndman, H.C., 122 E. 3rd (L)
SPRINGDALE
Elmer, Chas. F. (Hdq)
SULPHUR SPRINGS
Henderson, C.C. (M)

CALIFORNIA
ALHAMBRA
Wieland, Roy N., 1721 Cedar St. (A)
ARCADIA
Bonar, Lester M., 634 Estrella Ave. (F)
Keim, Thurman, E., 62 Pamela (Sup)
BEVERLY HILLS
Hilton, E.G., 801 N. Elm Dr. (Hdq)
CHOCHILLA
Pedretti, Ben, RFD (L)
COMPTON
Depew, Andy, 319 S. Sloan (B)
Whitaker, G.F., Box 191 (Sup)
CORCORAN
Beasley, Arthur (E)
Boss, H.L., 1014 Hall Ave. (Hdq)
CORNING
Camden, Otto O., Box 293 (H)
EAGLE ROCK
Prindle, Marshall E., 2750 Glenn Rock Ave. (I)
EL MONTE
Dirkson, Henry, 1328 N. Cogswell Rd. (Hdq)
Polona, Joe, 640 Lambert Ave. (K)
FULLERTON
Tilzey, Howard M., 331 W. Wilshire (B)
HANFORD
Royer, E.G., 410 W. 8th (L)
HOLLISTER
Cooper, L.A., 363 7th St. (MG)
HUNTINGTON PARK
Humphrey, W.C., 2634 Hope St. (D)
INGLEWOOD
Breitweg, Wm. J., 1006 E. 67th (A)
LAGUNA BEACH
Bell, R.L., 577 Lombardy Lane (F)

CALIFORNIA *(continued)*
LONG BEACH
Henry, Bert C., 3217 E. 4th (H)
Karstetter, J.B., 127 W. Mountain View (MG)
Parmenter, Clifford A., 4500 Harvey Way (MG)
LOS ANGELES
Blakey, V.B., 401 S. Spring St. (I)
Burr, E.R., 3628 Washington Blvd. (Amb)
Blumenthal, A., 546 N. Sierra Bonita (F)
Cohen, Sam A., 1042 S. Bedford (L)
Collins, Alex L., 2601 Santa Barbara Blvd. (MG)
Fletcher, Harold B., 128 W. Gage (Hdq)
Giesner, Herbert L., 2007 W. 80th (A)
Greer, Emmett L., 903 S. Lake (Amb)
Grimmer, G.R., 3231 Arvia St. (M) (I)
Laslett, Howard P., 4929 Highland View Ave., Eagle Rock (Hdq)
Lutz, E.A., 616-1/2 W. 35th Place (Hdq)
Nelson, Joseph N., 2023 W. 79th (A)
Shpall, Nimon, 1513-1/2 Pico Blvd. (K)
Wiles, Otis M., 1816 W. 42nd (B)
Woodward, Lloyd C., 642 Imogene (I-G)
Yaqubian, Aaron, 1150 Bonnie Beach Place (K)

MODESTO
Glass, Robert W., 338 Yosemite Ave. (I)
ONTARIO
Tweed, Jerry, 657 W. G St. (A)
PALO ALTO
Noll, John J., Box 784 (Hdq)
PASADENA
Chipman, Floyd A., 81 W. Peoria (B)
Douglas, Raymond W., 323 N. Euclid Ave. (A)
POMONA
Casey, Hal, Redwoos Inn (Hdq)
Conwill, Lloyd L., 377 McKinley (D)
Walker, Johnston E., 130 Monroe St. (D)
REDONDO BEACH
Singer, O.F., 315 N. Gertrude (K)
SACRAMENTO
Thayer, Frank, 528 14th St. (Sup)
SAN DIEGO
Gertisen, John, 1127 4th Ave. (E)
Morrison, Roy L., 3745 Grim Ave. (Hdq)
Moot, Clyde P., 4062 Central Ave. (Hdq)
Skelley, Geo A., 2969 Kalmia (Hdq)
Tvedt, Elmer T., 4023 Illinois (H)
Underwood, R.J., 1906 31st (K)

SAN FRANCISCO
Bailey, Morton, 2905 Russ Bldg. (MG)
Schmedinghoff, F.A., 136 Serano Dr. (A)
SAN GABRIEL
Flowers, C.B., 1936 Fairview Ave. (B)
Vial, Bert R., 906 Garibaldi (MG)
SAN MARINO
Whitson, Dr. Oscar, 1690 Rubio Dr. (Hdq)
SANTA ANNA
Harri, Gus, 1418 Maple Ave. (G)
Wellington, M.B., Bank of America Bldg. (I)
SANTA BARBARA
Cook, Geo H., 1118 Chapalo (Hdq)
TARZANA
Keck, R.P., 5808 Melvin Ave. I)
VENTURA
Slagle, Lynn E., 116 S. Pacific (L)

COLORADO
ARRIBA
Eberle, Lawrence W. (B)
AURORA
Enyart, John V., 1270 Dallas (Sup)
Farnish, Harry T., 11710 E. Fairfax Ave. (E)
BOULDER
Culver, Jas. O., 2156 Grove (H)
CRAIG
Davidson, F.A. (C)
Judd, Shirley M. (Sup)
COLORADO SPRINGS
Blick, Floyd A., 117 N. Logan (M)
Bock, John G., 3165 W. Colorado (M)
Carlson, Geo. A., 21 E. Washington (A)
Centlivre, Henry, 225 E. Jefferson (F)
Graham, Jas. H., 329 S. Wahsatch (A)
Harrisberger, A.B., 2122 N. Tejon St. (B)
Odgers, W.E., 318 S. Cascade (M)
Schick, John A., 720 E. Platte (Sup)
Todd, Bruce H., 1230 N. Corona St. (F)
Wallace, R.R., 402 N. Wahsatch Ave. (M)
DELTA
Austen, Oscar H., Box 52 (F)
DENVER
Bedwell, Clarence E., 1337 California (F)
DeBoer, Fred C., 678 E. 4th Ave. (A)
Dienst, Chas F., 1430 Zenoble (G)
Drennon, Earl, 1436 16th St. (M)
Earnhardt, A.B., 40 S. Fox (Hdq)
Gail, Walter August, 1295 Ash St. (D)

CALIFORNIA, Denver *(continued)*
 Goebel, Wm. R., 1440 High (H) Bldg.
  (F)
 Jordan, Elwood, 10329 E. Colfax (D)
 Kellogg, Hugh B., 806 E & C Bldg. (D)
 Lorig, Julius E., 840 Adams St. (K)
 Miller, David R., 1336 Gaylord St. (C)
 Mitchell, Arden H., 2650 S. Marion (M)
 Mitchell, Columbus N., 221 E. 3rd (I)
 Morrison, L.R., 840 Harrison St. (E)
 Plotkin, I., 1408 Larimer (M)
 Rieger, Francis F., 1414 Monroe (B)
 Smead, Burton A., 1281 S. Downing (E)
 Stender, Royal T., 239 Bonnock St. (Hdq)
 Sturdevant, Ralph E., 33007 Humboldt
  (Hdq)
 Temple, Oscar W., 210 Vine St. (K)
 Weil, Ralph E., 418 E. Mississippi (A)
ELIZABETH
 Tanin, William (L)
ENGLEWOOD
 Brooks, Dallas J., 3196 S. Logan (E)
FORT GARLAND
 Atencio, Alberto, Box 4 (L)
GRAND JUNCTION
 Biggs, Clyde H., 304 W. Main (Hdq)
 Hardin, John W., RFD 4 (E)
GREAT DIVIDE
 Finney, Chas E. (D)
GREELEY
 Snowberger, John, 1441 10th (D)
HOLYOKE
 Bennett, Glenn E. (F)
LAFAYETTE
 Pillmore, Edison A. (F)
LAJUNTA
 Rizzuto, Louis, 1001 Cimarron Ave. (L)
LAMAR
 Czapanskiy, Wm. F., 211 S. 9th (H)
LAS ANIMAS
 Corner, John R., 628 Elm (I)
 Kimble, Anton J., Kazan Route (L)
LAWSON
 Anderson, Walter E. (F)
LEADVILLE
 Bond, Eugene A., 16-16 Bank Annex
  Bldg. (E)
 Tullee, Frank, 320 Elm St. (A)
LONGMONT
 Cain, Turner, 337 9th Ave. (Sup)
 Young, Geo. L., 344 Vivian (G)
LITTLETON
 Dimond, Alben A., Route 1, Box 67 (H)

MANITOU
 Suttmoeller, J.C., 212 Midland (Hdq)
PRITCHETT
 Williamson, Leonard (K)
PUEBLO
 Easter, Elmer J., 423 Colorado Bldg. (G)
 Spencer, Walter G., 725 W. Grant (A)
ROCKY FORD
 Johnston, Geo F., 406 N. 9th (I)
SHERIDAN LAKE
 Ashley, Roy E. (H)

FLORIDA
ATLANTIC BEACH
 Petersen, M.C., Box 472 (MG)
COCOA
 Bailey, Wm. H., 1716 Manor Dr. (M)
LAKE WALES
 Draper, Henry E., 202 Stuart Ave. (C)
ST. PETERSBURG
 Peatross, Jas. L., 3583 Granada Way (F)

GEORGIA
SAVANNAH
 Paschal, Boykin, c/o Morning News (MG)
ATLANTA
 Decker, Gilbert S., 54 Ellis N.E. (F)
 Greenwood, A.E., Georgian Terrace Ho-
  tel (E)
 Reeves, Gen. James H., 307 2nd Ave.,
  S.E. (Fld)

IDAHO
EMMETT
 Dillon, Merle E. (H)
FILER
 Hawkins, L.W., RFD 1 (Bd)
MARSING
 Stafford, James G. (A)

ILLINOIS
BARRINGTON
 Berghorn, Wilbur (C)
 Olson, Thomas C., RFD 1 (MG)
BRADFORD
 Ames, James A. (E)
 Reed, Glenn E., RFD 2 (D)
BROADLANDS
 Dewitt, Hugo T. (Hdq)
CARTHAGE
 Agnew, Henry G. (E)
CHICAGO
 Derango, Eugene, 1007 S. Hamilton Ave.
  (L)

ILLINOIS, Chicago *(continued)*

Fox, Dr. Chas. M., 335 N. Menard St. (Med)

Falk, Fred C., 1531 Augusta Blvd. (H)

Kuss, F.W., 2748 Hampden Court (L)

Reesch, Peter J., 5623 S. Oakley Ave. (M)

Trnka, Frank, 1514 S. Keeler (H)

EAST DUBUQUE

Maire, Leslie J., Lock Box 15 (L)

ELGIN

Benthuysen, Wm. H., 103 S. Edison Ave. (G)

Lamprecht, E., 1002 Bellvue Ave. (G)

Lehman, Myron M., 23 Douglas Ave. (C)

Magden, Arthur H., 70 Lovell (G)

Middleton, Arthur H., 310 Ann St. (D)

ELMHURST

Cedarholm, Harold E., 586 Mitchell (Sup)

Semple, A.N., 437 Elm (Hdq)

ESSEX

Veronda, D.J. (E)

FISHER

Murray, Jordan S. (M)

FOREST PARK

Jennings, Harry, 1053 Dunlope Ave. (H)

GALVA

Fahnstrom, Elmer (F)

HIGHLAND PARK

Selfridge, Frank F., 27 N. Linden Ave. (MG)

Zipoy, Frank J., 736 S. St. John Ave. (I)

JOY

Mueller, Henry J., RFD 2 (H)

LASALLE

Stelmach, Frank, 1463 Zinc St. (K)

OAK PARK

Boeckelman, W.F., 846 N. Taylor (E)

Towne, Claude, 405 South Blvd. (G)

RUTLAND

Bendin, Alfred E. (C)

SILVIS

McCullough, R., 917 4th Ave. (G)

SPRINGFIELD

Huff, Dr. Elmer L., 230-1/2 S. 6th (I)

STERLING

MacLennan, Jos. M.J., 1310 First Ave. (C)

WHEATON

Weltner, John M., 807 N. Main St. (H)

WINSLOW

Rackow, Arthur R. (D)

INDIANA

LAFAYETTE

Barnes, Hugh R., State Soldiers Home (E)

IOWA

CARSON

Colwell, Everett L. (Med)

COUNCIL BLUFFS

Ford, R.V., 700 S. Main St. (D)

FT. MADISON

Snowden, L.A., 2412 Ave. M (Sup)

MASON CITY

Strickland, Chas E., Box 481 (M)

SIOUX CITY

Reed, Fred G., 2609 S. Cedar St. (H)

KANSAS

ABBYVILLE

Webster, Wm. A. (B)

ABILENE

Strowig, H.F., 407 Vine (L)

AGRA

Keckley, Elvin E. (E)

Molzahn, JOE C., RFD 1, Box 40 (E)

ALEXANDER

Thompson, Frank A. (K)

ALLEN

Jensen, George L. (L)

ALMA

Diehl, Wm., RFD 3 (L)

Hauer, Charles (E)

Rice, Frank (L)

Zwanziger, Martin (A)

ALMENA

Baird, Harry W., RFD 1 (D)

Van De Wege, Teanus (M)

ALTAMONT

Campbell, Winfield P., RFD 2 (I)

Traster, Ralph E. (Hdq)

ALTON

Wineland, Clyde C. (C)

AMERICUS

Bruce, Marshall (K)

AMES

Kieffer, Charles (M-MG)

ANTHONY

Keeble, Melvin, 318 S. Bluff Ave. (E)

Shaw, William D. (A)

White, William E. (A)

ARCADIA

Thompson, William (D)

ARKANSAS CITY

Derry, Harry A., RFD 4 (A)

Eagan, Cecil E., 514 S. D St. (G)

Mitchell, Charles, RFD 2 (C)

Munyon, C.I., RFD 3 (K)

Stahl, Ed H., 111 N. B St. (Hdq)

KANSAS *(continued)*

ASHLAND
Reed, George R. (D)

ATCHISON
Barnes, John C., RFD 1, Box 379 (I)
Begley, Leo M., RFD 3 (C)
Childs, Alonzo C., 505 Atchison St. (I)
Cummings, Jas., 716-1/2 Commercial (G)
Falk, H.A., RFD 2 (I)
Jackson, John S., Branchton (I)
Kaufman, John A., 1021 N. 2nd (Sup)
Killarney, Earl, 717 3rd St. (Sup)
Knowles, J. Ross, 824 Santa Fe St. (Sup)
Leak, Warren D., 1021 S. 9th St. (I)
Leight, Wm. F., 1652 Commercial (I)
Lorenz, Joe, 708 N. 2nd St. (I)
McCourt, John W., RFD 1 (I)
Meyer, Claude L., 821 S. 5th St. (I)
O'Connor, E.T., 1428 Santa Fe. (MG)
Ross, Frank C., 310 Riley (H)
Schaeffer, Edwin L., 1307 Div. St. (I)
Smith, L.A., 1025 Parallel (I)
Stuebinger, Walter, 308 Commercial (Med)
Stumpf, Frank F., 109 S. 16th St. (I)
Sullivan, Ed., 108 Atchison (I)
Tabor, Chas. Lee (I)
Turner, Courtney S., 1135 Commercial (Hdq)

ATLANTA
Holt, Curtis K., RFD 2 (G)

ATWOOD
Heble, Rudolph A., RFD 2 (Sup)
Samson, Arthur J. (Sup)

AUBURN
Andrew, Kelly (MG)
Madden, Paul, 140 Harrison St. (MG)
AUGUSTA
Liouia, E.P. (Sup)

AXTELL
Magill, W.F. (L)

BAILEYVILLE
Gockel, Frank J. (H)

BARNARD
Cramb, Will (C)

BARNES
Fagan, Raymond (M)

BAXTER SPRINGS
Armstrong, Jas. B., 1029 Military (H)
McKenzie, Ralph W., 311 E. 7th St. (H)
Wade, Clyde, 141 N. Willow (D)

BAZINE
Olson, Carey (F)

BEATTIE
Heeney, Barney (K)

BELLAIRE
Post, Dave (H)

BELLE PLAINE
Duvall, Walter L. (D)

BELLEVILLE
Doctor, George Jack, RFD 1 (F)
Everhart, Frank, 1106 O St. (F)

BELOIT
Bourbon, Oliver J., RFD 1 (A)
Foote, L.E., 506 N. Mill (A)
Kethcart, Oral W., 515 N. Pine (M)
Severance, Robt. J., 319 Western (A)

BERN
Strahn, Andy (A)

BETHEL
Kane, Alva (Med)
Landell, D., RFD 1 (Sup)
Scamahorn, RFD 1 (Sup)

BEVERLY
Donbarger, Arthur (I)

BIRD CITY
Leitner, Wm. (K)
Powell, Edd L., RFD 1 (Hdq)

BISON
Degenhardt, Jacob (L)
Gisick, Henry (M)
Schwartzkopf, Fred. R. (Hdq)

BLUE MOUND
Spotts, James (Sup)

BLUFF CITY
Cook, Alvin (E)
Schmidt, H.N. (Hdq)

BOGUUE
Metheny, John J. (Hdq)

BREWSTER
Bear, Earl D. (M)

BROOKVILLE
Vogan, George E. (F)

BROWNELL
Pierce, Edward E. (F)
Rourke, John J., RFD 1 (MG)

BUCKLIN
Weikal, Ralph E. (Hdq)

BUNKER HILL
Letesch, John H. (Sup)

BURDEN
Anderson, James (G)

BURLINGAME
Masters, Weaver L., RFD 3 (L)

BURLINGTON
Vincent, Carl, 1020 Niagra (K)

BURNS
  Knausman, Theodore F. (D)
BUSHTON
  Boldt, Fred (MG)
  Voss, Chris F., RFD 1 (H)
  West, H.M., RFD 1 (C)
CALDWELL
  Bothwell, Wm. E., 324 N. Osage (E)
  Keown, Wilbur D., 219 N. Webb (H)
  Smock, James M., RFD 3 (D)
CANEY
  Adams, Clarence C., 402 S. State
  Erard, Earl (C)
  Kennedy, Lester L. (G) (Hdq)
CANTON
  Bryan W.C., RFD 1 (A)
CARBONDALE
  Mercer, Claude S. (F)
  Waetzig, William (B)
  Weil, Marshall W. (F)
CAWKER CITY
  Mildrexer, Joseph S. (D)
  Suter, J.R., RFD 1 (1)
  Thille, Fred (A)
CHAPMAN
  Delker, Henry (K)
CHARDON
  Myers, Robert (D)
CHERRYVALE
  Hucke, John F., RFD 3 (K)
  Slaybaugh, Floyd F., 309 Whelan (D)
  Wilks, Wm. E., RFD 2 (K)
CIMARRON
  Hesler, Jesse C. (Hdq)
CLAFLIN
  Kukula, Charles A. (L)
CLEARWATER
  Macredie, Alex L. (F)
  Senter, Ray (E)
CLYDE
  Beneda, Frank (H)
  Chartier, Perl D. (E)
  Koch, John P., RFD 1 (E-MG)
  LeBarge, Homer L. (Sup)
COATS
  Chastain, Willard (H)
COFFEYVILLE
  Custer, Leroy F. (G)
  Harer, C.G., 106 E. 8th (D)
  Johnson, Elliott O., 303 Walnut (L)
  Kimberlin, H.W., RFD 4 (Hdq)
  Livingston, Ray, 304 E. 12th (C)

  Schott, Paul J., 1100 Willow (H)
  Station, Edward, 716 E. 10th (E)
  Wade, Connel, 904 W. 5th St. (D)
  Ward, Leo S., 1601 Maple St. (Hdq)
COLBY
  Bellamy, Clarence (M)
  Dawes, John C. RFD 2 (D)
  Hunn, Frank L., Box 355 (Med)
  Nahrung, Carl, RFD 2 (K)
COLLYER
  Maliowsky, Frank V. (MG)
  Tomonek, F.F. (I)
COLONY
  Lewis, Ralph C. (K)
  Myers, Fred L., RFD 3 (E)
COLUMBUS
  Best, Lee F., 410 S. Vermont (G)
  Blincoe, Claude, Box 73 (A)
  Bull, Harry O., RFD 3 (D)
  Elliott, Floyd A., 326 6th Ave. (G)
  Hanshay, Claude R., 305 N. Ohio (L)
  Holland, Frank, RFD 3 (H)
  Masterson, E.J., 408 Lynn St. (Sup)
  Smith, Wm. C., 723 E. Walnut (D)
CONCORDIA
  Bowling, Walter, 836 E. 7th St. (E)
  Cook, Harrison R., 137-1/2 E. 10th (H)
  Culbertson, Carey H., 602 W. 10th St.
    (L)
  Holding, Edwin, 1203 Broadway (Hdq)
  Johnston, Lawrence (E)
  Lawson, Edwin, 720 E. 10th St. (C)
  Maloney, Gus, 432 E. 6th (H)
  Shrader, G.V. (Sup)
CONWAY
  Mishler, Vernie S. (Sup)
COTTONWOOD FALLS
  Meyers, Irving (D)
COUNCIL GROVE
  Carr, John B., 922 Welch St. (I)
  Crawford, B.H. (Med)
  Marlett, Harry G., 113 Railroad Ave. (I)
CULVER
  Pruett, Ralph, RFD 1 (M)
DEERFIELD
  Bechtel, William E. (F)
  London, H.D. (Hdq)
DELPHOS
  Bourne, Bert H. (Hdq)
DENSMORE
  Boys, Ralph R. (H)
  Conklin, W.T. (F)
  Voss, Louis J. (F)

DENTON
Burke, C.L. (K)
Ramsiere, Everett (K)
Schupe, James (K)
Streator, F.D. (K)

DERBY
Sickler, Henry W. (E)

DE SOTO
Kueker, Fred L., Box 131 (A)
Longstreth, Guy V. (Hdq)

DEVON
Post, Roy (D)

DIGHTON
Felix R. (A)

DILLON
Heller, Milu, Elmo (M)

DODGE CITY
Brown, E.A., 605 W. Chestnut St. (Sup)
Burkholder, Wm. M., Box 1079 (Hdq)
Calloway, A.B., 1715 Ave. A (I)
Clinton, C.L., 1000 First Ave. (E)
Partridge, Ray, 116 Market (C)
Wilson, O.R., 708 West A (D)

DOUGLASS
Piper, Olave (Hdq)
Winson, Bert, RFD (D)

DRESDEN
Karls, Michael J. (L)
Marcuson T.A., RFD 2 (A)
Tice, Glenn (Sup)

EASTON
Fevurly, Grover F. (MG)
Kreutzer, John (L)

EDNA
Smith, Albert, RFD 2 (L)

EFFINGHAM
Meador, Clarence (I)
Schaefer, Chas. H. (I)
Stutz, C.F. (I)
Wilson, Arth (MG)

EL DORADO
Cochran, R.C., 210 W. Central (A)
Ellis, Erle G., 123 N. Arthur (D)
Gilmore, Benj. H., RFD 4 (D)

ELK FALLS
Morton, R.G. (B)

ELKHART
Zimmerman, Bert R. (A)

ELLIS
Slaughter, Milo, 103 W. Franklin (F)
Underhill, S.M. (Hdq)
Weisner, Frank A., RFD 1 (C)

ELLSWORTH
Eklund, Isadore C. (L)
Holt, William R. (M)
McCoy, Chas. (K)
Mylnar, Louis (K)
Shoemaker, Harry J. (A)
Ulrickson, Frank (K)
Wilson, Levi V. (K)

ELMO
Heller, Milt, P.O. Dillon (M)

EMMETT
Trezise, Reuben (G)

EMPORIA
Bogue, Ray, 931 Oak St. (A)
Duncan, Clyde W., 127 W. 7th (I)
Groh, Jonas L., 1326 Lawrence St. (A)
Mole, S.E., 1009 Neosho St. (C)
Montgomery, Gilliard S., RFD 5 (D)
Toms, Abe, RFD 3 (F)
Ulm, Walter E., RED 3 (F)
Worley, C.S., 626 Lincoln St. (Hdq)

ENTERPRISE
Lungstrom, Harry L. (Jack) (Hdq)

ESKRIDGE
Logan, W.R. (L)
Wyre, B.H. (L)

EUDORA
McCoy, S.E. (A)

FARLINGTON
Martinson, Albert N., RFD 1 (MG)

FLORENCE
Scherer, John H., Box 7 (E)

FONTANA
Vermillion, Ben (D)

FORMOSA
Cunningham, Otie R. (E)

FORT DODGE
Beamer, Walter G. (B)
Herdman, Wm. (B)
Spencer, Homer (Amb)

FORT SCOTT
Dugan, John I., RFD 5 (B)
Hill, Carl F., 1123 S. Main (K-Hdq)
Johnson, Lucas H., 322 S. Eddy (B)
Keeney, Perry L., RFD 4 (MG)
Swain, Claude L., 821 S. Crawford St. (MG)
Wells, Robert L., 1224 Judson (C)

FRANKFORT
Gudenkauf, H.G. (G)

FREDONIA
Adkins, Chester (Amb)
Criswell, Ralph (Amb)
Duncan, Dr. E.C. (Amb)

KANSAS, Fredonia *(continued)*
    Grooner, N.E. (Amb)
    Ingles, Wm. (Amb)
    Ramsey, Burke (Amb)
    Verchere, Charlie, 108 N. 11th St. (Amb)
    Wells, Leslie (Amb)
FRONTENAC
    Friskel, John C., P.O. Box 186 (D)
GALVA
    Nelson, W.M., RFD (I)
GARDEN CITY
    Cook, A.E., 624 N. 11th (Hdq)
    Griffin, Wm. A., 1112 5th St. (D)
    Metz, Chas T., 601 James Ave. (F)
    Payne, Earl T., 305 N. 5th (I)
    Smith, Leonard P., Machine Sup. Co. (D)
    Walls, Claire M. (B)
GARLAND
    Albright, Dr. Fred C. (Med)
GARNETT
    Archer, Ralph D., Rm. 1, Kirk Bldg. (C)
    Bronston, Jason L., 317 W. 6th Ave. (M)
GENESEO
    Dolezal, James (I)
    Handlin, Wm. B. (K)
GIRARD
    Veatch, W. Frank (Amb)
GLASCO
    Bourne, Bert H. (Hdq)
    Capron, A.E. (E)
GLEN ELDER
    Daugherty, Hiram, RFD 2 (A)
    Eberle, Leo H. (B)
    Humes, Edwin A. (E)
    Norris, Ernest W. (Hdq)
GODDARD
    Schoenecker, John J., RFD 1 (Sup)
GOODLAND
    Bigler, Chas L. (F)
    Erickson, E.A. (F)
    Golden, Reed H. (I)
GRANTVILLE
    Chalmers, Robert (Hdq)
GREAT BEND
    Brough, Leroy I., 1915 Madison (I)
    Capes, Jess, 1614 Madison (Hdq)
    Robertson, Alfred C., Hotel Zarah (MG)
    Schlegel, Edward, 1112 Williams (K)
    Whitacre, Joseph A., 2514 Eleventh St. (K)
GREELEY
    Grove, Kenneth (M)
    Lickteig, Philip, RFD 1 (M)
    Rommelfanger, Wm. J. (MG)

GREENLEAF
    Ruoff, Christy H. (L)
GREENSBURG
    Allensworth, C.O. (G)
GRENOLA
    Thompson, R.J. (Hdq)
GRIDLEY
    Miller, Henry E., Box 208 (MG)
HALSTEAD
    Schowalter, M.M., 303 Poplar (G)
    Westfall, Dr. George (Med)
HANOVER
    Kile, Ed (L)
HARPER
    Coulson, E.N., 111 W. 14th (E)
    Minger, John W. (E)
HARVEYVILLE
    Kopp, W.C. (L)
HAVEN
    Hill, Cleve (MG)
    Miller, Emil (C)
    Scott Fred (K)
    Wick, Ted F. (F)
HAVENSVILLE
    Booth, Henry (Sup)
HAYS
    Hauschild, H.A. (L)
    Wentworth, Ray, 510 W. 15th (L)
HIAWATHA
    Gregg, Albert B., RFD 4 (K)
    Patton, Harry (M)
HIGHLAND
    Blevins, J.D. (K)
    Franklin, Frances (Hdq)
HILL CITY
    Hull, Frederick L., RFD 2 (M)
HOISINGTON
    Stock, Glenn, 263 W. 4th (H)
HOLLENSBERG
    Brennis, Carl E. (L)
    Gustin, Jesse S. (M)
HOLTON
    Bhear, George M. (E)
    Hahn, George S. (F)
    Miller, Arthur W., Box 345 (K)
HOLYROOD
    Murray, Wm. A.B. (Hdq)
HORTON
    Freeland, James P., RFD 1 (I)
    Thornton, Vernie L., RFD 1 (I)
HOWARD
    Cummins, Arthur W., RFD 2 (B)
    Gill, E.A. (Hdq)
    Heater, Monroe D., RFD 2 (Hdq)

KANSAS, Howard *(continued)*

Perkins, Ralph (B)
Thompson, Paul M. B)

HOXIE
Clinesmith, Jacob H. C)
Morse, Fred E., Box 216 (B)

HUMBOLDT
Wolf, Lee, RFD 1 (H)

HUNTER
Kock, George E. (Sup)

HURON
Black, G.F., Gen. Delivery (I)

HUTCHINSON
Bartlett, Russell, 728 E. 10th (A)
Bates, Chester I., 115 E. 12th (A)
Bivins, F.A., 811 E. 9th (A)
Brack, J., 514 N. Maple (E)
Bryant, Bill, 304 W. C (A)
Eby, Don, 807 N. Adams (B)
Frost, Roy M., Box 469 (E)
Holdren, B.F., 114 N. Plum St. (I)
Hoy, Dale, 524 E. 1st (C)
Hughes, John C., 829 E. B (Hdq)
Hunt, Sam L., 600 E. Sherman (C)
Long, Vernon L., 10 W. 14th St. (Hdq)
Moyer, R.C., 421 E. 9th St. (C)
Randles, Eugene S., 123 W. 22nd (A)
Rea, R.C., 815 N. Maple (D)
Robinson, J.L., Wolcott Barber Shop (H)
Sanders, L.E., 1716 N. Poplar (Sup)
Schonholtz, L.C., 1124 W. 11th St. (Hdq)
Sheddan, M.F., RFD 3 (H)
Shurtz, H.B., 4 E. 19th (Sup)
Sloan, Jas L., 3 E. Sherman (D)
Veatch, Chauncey L., 107 N. Walnut (Amb)
Waggoner, Herbert, 4 W. 22nd (Amb)
Welch, Perry A., 108 W. 20th (Amb)

INDEPENDENCE
Constant, W.J., 122 N. Penn (Amb)
Nelson, J.W., 808 E. Popular (E)
Zimmerman, C.C., 319 S. 10th St. (Hdq)

INMAN
Haydon, Lester F. (Sup)

IOLA
Stout, Cecil J., 405 S. Jefferson (B)
Whitehead, R.W., 304 West St. (I)

IRVING
Choffee, W.M. (F)

JAMESTOWN
Smith, Ralph W., RFD 2 (Sup)

JENNINGS
Tacha, Frank W. (Sup)

JETMORE
Pitts, Ray T. (Hdq)

JOHNSON
Josserand, Orvine E. (Hdq)

JUNCTION CITY
Heck, T.A., 220 W. Spruce (Hdq)
Humphrey, J.V., Jr., 916 N. Washington (K)
O'Donnell, Dr. F.W. (Med)
Westfall, Walter E., 512 W. 4th St. (Hdq)
Woodford, Mark M., P.O. Box 355 (F)

KANAPOLIS
Hudson, Leonard M., RFD 2 (K)
Sanders, Oscar (Hdq)

KANONA
Janousek, Fred, Box 123 (Hdq)

KANORADO
Magnus, Alva D. (H)

KANSAS CITY
Barrett, Wm. H. (w) 3015 Parkwood Blvd. (A)
Bauer, August, 1014 Haskell (M)
Button, Joseph M., 748 Washington Blvd. (Hdq)
Calvert, Wm. C., 2067 N. 13th St. (Med)
Collins, Carl L., 2629 Armstrong (C)
Cross, Walter P., 1603 Metropolitan Ave. (Sup)
Erie, Francis A., 1630 S. 42nd St. (MG)
Ferguson, Roy A., 3146 Lafayette (C)
Fiederling, Harry, 1917 Sloan (K)
Gribbin, C.S., 1819 Quindaro (MG)
Hankinson, W., 2701 Wood (MG)
Harvey, Wm. A., 2211 Wood Ave. (G)
Hoff, Leo J., 1844 Quindaro (M)
Jones, F.F., 4905 Leavenworth Rd. (Hdq)
Kane, H.J., 274 N. 6th St. (I)
Latchem, Clyde, 8th and Ann Apts. (MG)
Leat, Frank W., 3055 Silver Ave. (Sup)
Mayswinkle, Lloyd, 2836 Hiawatha (I)
McMahon, Clarence A., 725 Tauromee (Sup)
Nation, W.R., 1716 Woodland (K)
Neel, Ward L., 329 N. 30th St. (K)
Nelson, Frank J., 4471 Adams St. (H)
Orrick, Homer T., 2842 Orville (MG)
Peters, Hugh P., 1901 Tauromee (B)
Pigman, Darrel L., 213 S. Coy (Hdq)
Quilty, Robert, 434 N. 29th St. (F)
Robinson, Henry W., 1517 Lawless (Hdq)
Schofield, W.C., 2226 Wood (M)
Smith, Orin G., 1809 Minnesota (IK)
Stimson, A.G., 3129 Delavan (L)

KANSAS, Kansas City *(continued)*
 Stuckker, L.L., 703 Central (E)
 Thorn (Howard H., 1209 N. 19th St. (A)
 Younghans, W.O., 1946 N. 30th (MG)
KENSINGTON
 Anthony, Dewey, Box 148 (H)
KINGMAN
 McRae, C.J. (G)
KINGSDOWN
 Haley, Velma S. (D)
KINSLEY
 Tew, Ernest (F)
KIOWA
 Cornwell, W.M., RFD 1 (I)
 Ikerd, L.D. (I)
KIRWIN
 Roman, Karl T. (Sup)
LACROSSE
 Jacobs, George (E)
 Renberger, Glen H. (H)
 Stang, Herman E. (Hdq)
LAMAR
 Freeman, Earl A. (H)
LANCASTER
 Gigstead, Harry, RFD 6 (I)
LANE
 White, N.D. (B)
LANSING
 Matthews, James (Hdq)
LARNED
 Shuss, Jake, 222 W. 5th (D)
LAWRENCE
 Bell, C.V., 844 Tennessee (Med)
 Bleisner, Clarence A., 747 Vermont,
  Police Dept. (C)
 Coleman, Clare J., RFD 1 (WW2)
 Hout, Thomas H., RFD 4 (L)
 Hurwitz, S.W., 202 W. 6th (D)
 Kendall, R. Rex, 1346 New Hampshire
  (C)
 McClain, Walt A., 2027 New Hampshire
  (K)
 Pasewark, W.H., 1926 Barker St. (I)
 Roy, V.W., 705 Maine (K)
 Schwann, S.E., Jayhawker Theater (H)
 Twente, J.W., 934 Indiana (Med)
LEAVENWORTH
 Cahill, Joseph J., 2100 Cherokee (C)
 Clark, Bentley, 523 Ohio St. (B)
 Downs, Arthur S., 323 Osage St. (B)
 Gordon, E.L., 507 Osage (H)
 Galvin, Daniel V., 616 Osage (B)
 Hashagen, August R., 1114 N. Broadway
  (C)

 Herkins, Joseph F., 317 S. 10th (H)
 Herrig, Anton, 313 Atlantic (C)
 Hewitt, Zell, c/o 324 Delaware (B)
 Hoy, Ed, 1308 Ottawa St. (B)
 Keiser, Albert, 504 Miami (C)
 Leinhardt, A.V., 805 Potts (B)
 McCaffrey, Jas. O., c/o 405 Cherokee (B)
 Melvin, Ray A., Rm. 27, P.O. Bldg. (E)
 Miller, Edward L., 788 Osage (G)
 Moore, John P., 800 Metropolitan (Sup)
 Peet, Groucher, 27 Rose (B)
 Werely, August, 714 Miami (B)
LEBANON
 Haxton, Frank W. (I)
 Klemm, D.F., Box 49 (E)
 Rice, L.E. (K)
LEBO
 Evans, Gwilym R., Lebo St. Bk. (F)
 Gahagan, Van (M)
LENEXA
 Phillips, A. (C)
 Yost, Carl M., 415 Third (MSG)
LEON
 Wright, Martin H., RFD 1 (A)
LEWIS
 Newlin, John S. (F)
LIBERAL
 Marshall, Robt. W. (Hdq)
LINCOLN
 Anderson, A.A. (D)
 Feldkamp, RFD 1, Box 84 (Sup)
 Montgomery, W.L., 118 W. Franklin (M)
 Sheets, Harry C., 308 W. Yauger (C)
LINDSBORG
 Adams, Earl J., FD 1 (Hdq)
 Dahlstrom, Carl W., 318 S. 2nd (B)
 Hagstrand, J.A. (Sup)
 Koons, Royal E. (Sup)
 Larson, Oscar R., 315 Harrison
 Reynolds, Albert, 303 N. Washington
  (H)
LINWOOD
 Reetz, Frederick (C)
LOGAN
 Baird, James (A)
LONG ISLAND
 Brees, John T. (E)
LONGTON
 Dame, Geo W. (B)
LOST SPRINGS
 Nelson, John W., RFD 1 (I)
LOUISBURG
 Masoner, Elmer (D)
 Phillips, Earl B., RFD 1 (D)

KANSAS *(continued)*
LOUISVILLE
  Schreiber, J.E. (L)
LUCAS
  Dickinson, C.E. (B)
  Kvasnicka, R.E. (HDQ)
LYONS
  Boroughs, Ruble, Box 496 (B)
  Jackson, Bronce (M)
  Winn, Waldo J. (K)
MACKSVILLE
  Bates, Ernest (F)
McCUNE
  Justice, Oscar L., RFD 2 (I)
  Roese, Karl (F)
  Rogers, Arthur L., RFD 1 (B)
McLOUTH
  Watson, Herman C. (B)
McPHERSON
  Bradshaw, M.C., 610 S. Walnut (Hdq)
  Bremyer, A.W. (Andy), 736 E. Marlin St. (G)
  Carlson, E., Box 594 (F)
  Coughenour, Glenn (Supp)
  Kubin, Jeff, 829 N. Elm (Sup)
  Stanley, Fred, P.O. Drawer 309, (Hdq)
  Peterson, Emil E. (D)
  West, Arby M., 718 N. Chestnut (H)
MADISON
  Fellay, Chester E. (I)
MANHATTAN
  Geffert, Andrew P., 400-A Poyntz (Hdq)
  Hoke, M.A., RFD 1 (F)
  Jackson, E.G., 1406 Houston (E)
  Keller, Ward, 1715 Fairview St. (E)
  Ryan, Chas. L., 1634 Laramie (WW2)
MANKATO
  Whitmer, Elmer (K)
MAPLE HILL
  Smith, Riley I., RFD 1 (D)
MAPLETON
  Hessong, Orvan M., RFD 1 (K)
MARION
  Kline, Harry R. (K)
MARQUETTE
  Hunsinger, Fritz (I)
  Larson, Luther M. (Sup)
MARYSVILLE
  Ford, Robert (D)
  Straub, John J., 303 Carolina (D)
MAYETTA
  Hale, Jack Cody (B)
  Robson, Chas F. (K)
  Wyatt, Robert S. (D)

MEADE
  Haskins, Guerald (B)
MEDICINE LODGE
  McCune, Winnie F. (C)
  Palmer, H.A. (Amb)
  Shell, Everett G. (Sup)
MERRIAM
  Blanton, Geo., 5910 Marylea Rd. (A)
  Steinmetz, Geo., 5525 Loomis Ave., R. 2 (A)
MILTONVALE
  Loyd, Stanley (B)
MINNEAPOLIS
  Anderson, John R. (K)
  Boner, Leslie L. (K)
  Cromley, Frank G. (G)
  Killiam, P.M. (Bruce) (Med)
  Lanapeneau, Geo. N., 112 N. Rothsay (A)
MOLINE
  Morrow, Alick (D)
MORLAND
  Richmeier, John J. (M)
MOUND CITY
  Dewey, Emery O. (M)
  Kenney, John Z. (Hdq)
MOUND VALLEY
  Bitsko, Michael K. (L)
MOUNT HOPE
  Caffery, Thomas B. (C)
MULBERRY
  Amaux, Ben, RFD 1 (A)
MULVANE
  Lindsey, Ralph C. (D)
  Rippel, F.A., Box 271 (I)
NAVARRE
  Lake, Clifford (Sup)
NEODESHA
  McCullough, C.A., 208 N. 8th (L)
NEWTON
  Fagan, Joseph J., 912 Plum St. (K)
NICKERSON
  Green, Rush J. (E)
NORTON
  Bower, Med G. (K)
  Donovan, John M., RFD 1 (F)
OAKLEY
  Tholen, Henry T. (Sup)
OBERLIN
  Bennet, Roy (C)
  Gardner, Geo. W., RFD 3 (F)
  Gierhart, Glen W. (A)
OKETO
  Kelley, William (C)

KANSAS *(continued)*
OLATHE
    Craig, Lloyd E. (Hdq)
    Jamison, W.E., RFD 3 (A)
    Walters, Albert, RFD 2 (A)
OLPE
    Hohne, Fred C. (A)
ONAGA
    Berges, Otto (E)
    Kelly, Lester (G)
OSAGE CITY
    Gillaspy, James T., 320 Holiday (I)
    Johnson, Carl H., 286 Lakin (Hdq)
OSAWATOMIE
    Bearly, S.D., 1231 Main (D)
    Day, Clarence H., RFD 2 (D)
    Dunaway, Dana L., 937 Main (D)
    Hinderlighter, Chas. N., Box 345 (D)
    Kearney, John H., P.O. Box 223 (I)
    Lease, George (D)
    Smith, Edgar W. (F)
OSBORNE
    Beck, John H. (A)
    Wade, J.G., 118 W. Adams (C)
OSWEGO
    Rife, Cash, 723 Illinois (E)
    Walker, Corby M. (D)
OTIS
    Scheuerman, Adam E. (E)
OTTAWA
    Drum, Guy, 604 Willow St. (G)
    Duvall, H.F., 228 S. Elm (E)
    Hegberg, Clarence W., 314 S. Elm (Sup)
    Knight, Grover, 916 S. Main (Hdq)
    McCullough, Ray M., RFD 3 (B)
    Park, Carl, Box 319 (K)
    Redmond, Roscoe R., 1144 S. Hickory St. (Hdq)
    Wineinberger, W.E., 112 S. Main (B)
OVERLAND PARK
    Earnshaw, J.H., 5510 W. 79th St. (L)
    Linde, Ralph S., 7924 Conser (Sup)
PAOLA
    Bonslaugh, Howard (A)
    DeTar, Jay, 106 E. Peoria St. (D)
    Guylee, George (D)
    Kelly, David, 302 W. 3rd (MG)
    Kennedy, W.G., RFD 2 (D)
    Kettler, Fred, RFD 4, Box 109 (D)
    Koehler, Leo (D)
    Manchester, Dwight, RFD 5, Box 44 (D)
    McDaniel, James J., 502 W. Wea (D)
    Moote, Edward T., 910 E. Peoria (D)
    Phillips, C.C., 605 E. Plankishaw (D)
    Whitaker, Robert A., 410 College (D)

PARK
    Ackerman, Henry G. (Hdq)
PARSONS
    Allison, F.H., 2309 Clark (A)
    Coker, A.R., 2115 Main st. (A)
    Dodds, L.A., 1013 S. 24th St. (L)
    Ervin, Claude H., 2027 Main (Hdq)
    Gardner, Ward A., 1330 Corning (F)
    Hindenach, Raymond P., 2200 Briggs Ave. (I)
    Simmons, Joseph R., 1708 Dirr (Hdq)
    Watson, Chas. H., 1209 Appleton (Hdq)
PAXICO
    Mock, Wm. V., RFD 1 (L)
PEABODY
    Johnston, Paul B., 807 Olive (K)
    Reid, Olen (D)
    Stovall, S.A., Box 526 (Sup)
PENOKEE
    Critchfield, Chas. M. (D)
    Goff, Ulysses S. (D)
    Moore, Ralph (M)
PERRY
    Williams, Leonard, RFD 2 (C)
PERU
    Cunningham, Guy, RFD 2 (MG)
    Lindsey, Paul J., Lock Box 306 (F)
PFEIFER
    Meder, George (L)
PITTSBURG
    Claypool, Homer C., 99 Wash., Apt. 5 (H)
    Davis, C.O., 412 W. Quincy (K-Sup)
    Davis, John Jr., 502 S. Broadway (Hdq)
    Manninger, Jesse, RFD 4 (Bd)
    O'Toole, M.F., 925 E. 7th (K)
    Tanner, A.L., 711 W. 8th (Hdq)
    Walche, Frank, 604 N. Grand (L)
PLAINVILLE
    Bland, Harley C. (E)
PLEASANTON
    Leisure, Wm. Bryan (I)
POMONA
    Burns, Ernest A. (E)
PRAIRIEVIEW
    Soodsma, Corneal (E)
PRATT
    Gilham, C.B. (H)
    Ladd, Fred, 412 W. 3rd (C)
    Meek, Fred C., 216 N. Jackson (Hdq)
    Neagle, Coakley T., 415 E. 5th (H)
    Norby, Oscar M., 207 S. Iuka (H)
    Scott, J.E. (H)
    Swisher, Oliver F., RFD 1 (H)

KANSAS *(continued)*

PRESTON
  Kirkwood, Lester G. (B)
PRETTY PRAIRIE
  Day, W.W., RFD 2 (Hdq)
QUINTER
  Johnson, Roy A. (Hdq)
RANSOM
  Doerschlod, W.A. (F)
RANTOUL
  Lehew, William F., RFD 1 (B)
REDWING
  Warner, Louis, RFD 1 (H)
REXFORD
  Woerpel, Frederick W., RFD 1 (Sup)
ROSSVILLE
  Cottle, Samuel H. (D)
ROXBURY
  Florine, Palmon J. (Hdq)
RUSH CENTER
  Shiney, Fred H. (C)
RUSSELL
  Banker, Louis W., 737-1/2 Main St. (Sup)
  Krug, Geo A., 1036 Maple (Hdq)
  Mitchell, Oscar R., RFD 1 (Hdq)
  Thoman, Roy S., 330 W. 7th (I)
SABETHA
  Hook, Hugh L., 1115 Main (I)
  Wilson, Goff (E)
  Wenger, Jacob L., RFD 4 (E)
ST. FRANCIS
  Mitchell, Hugh (MG)
ST. PAUL
  Owens, John A. (M)
SALINA
  Baxendale, G.E., 800 State (D)
  Brown, Joel L., 612 W. South (M)
  Herman, Walter, 1108 Johnstown (M)
  Hodgson, Owen E., 660 Highland (B)
  Holtberg, Arthur T., 833 Sheridan (H)
  Miller, A.H., 629 Santa Fe (H)
  Nyberg, H.E. (John), 930 S. 5th (M)
  Ribble, A.E., 704 N. Santa Fe (Sup)
  Smith, Harry, 412 E. Antrim (A)
  Stafford, Elmer, 613 N. 13th (I)
  Van Liew, Charles L., 308 S. 5th (M)
  Vogan, H.L., 312 N. 11th (F)
  Vogelsburg, Mathias, 975 Highland (F)
  Young, George W., 220 W. 10th (L)
SATANTA
  Foster, Herbert (MG)
SAWYER
  Cole, H.E. (H)

SCAMMON
  McCormick, Daniel P. (H)
  Pattinson, Thomas (Hdq)
SCANDIA
  Thompson, Michael, RFD 1 (Sup)
SCOTT CITY
  Doyle, J.H., 604 W. 6th (D)
  Morris, E.P. (Hdq)
SCOTTSVILLE
  Cox, Carl A. (A)
SCRANTON
  Barlow, Charles R. (E)
  Eklund, C.V. (MG)
  Hug, Frank E. (MG)
  Martin, Sidney B. (E)
  Michaels, James M. (D)
  Rowe, W.H., RFD 1 (F)
SEDAN
  Funk, Ben J. (C)
  Kinneman, Will (G)
  Snair, Arnold (H)
SENECA
  Tate, Charles A., 1006 Roanoke (Hdq)
SEVERANCE
  Fenely, Franklin (K)
  Halling, August (K)
  Moser, Harry (K)
SEVERY
  Songer, Harry O. (D)
SHARON
  Coleman, V.G. (MG)
SHARON SPRINGS
  Bowen, Iris A. (A)
SHIELDS,
  Bryant, Marion (F)
SILVER LAKE
  Bridgeford, John F. (D)
  Brooks, Samuel R. (H)
  Brown, G.W. (E)
  McRoberts, George (I)
  Parr, L.O. (H)
SIMPSON
  Lockard, James W. (G)
SMITH CENTER
  Kinyon, Joe (H)
  Werts, Jack (B)
SPIVEY
  Manjoet, Wm. (D)
SPRING HILL
  Gay, James E. (A)
SOUTH HAVEN
  Hutchinson, Bernel D. (E)
STERLING
  Brock, E.R., Brock Drug Store (H)

STRONG CITY
Park, Carl (K)

SUBLETTE
Nilson, D.S. (E)

SUMMERFIELD
Volle, Lee A. (L)

SUN CITY
Bullock, A.L. (I)

SYLVAN GROVE
Walback, Clyde B. (Sup)

SYLVIA
Crandall, Cecil C., RFD 2 (I)

TECUMSEH
Morris, Robert O. (Hdq)

TONGANOXIE
Anderson, Ray (B)
Angell, Ivan (L)
Klinkenberg, E.G., RFD 2 (C)

TOPEKA
Billings, D.R., 1511 Webster (L)
Brown, Fred, 1216 Clay (Sup)
Casey, Leroy, 1801 Seabrook Ave. (Sup)
Coop, Harry M., 108 Winter (G)
Dalton, Thos. I., 405 Hillside (G)
DeBord, Bermin E., 505 Buchanan (G)
Doud, L.V., 621 Jackson (D)
Dyatt, W.L., 1123 Horne (M)
Fisher, Dale, c/o St. Tax Com. (MG)
Hinshaw, Glenn P., 526 Washburn (C)
Horton, S.J., 2101 N. Kansas (Sup)
Jenkins, S.K., 317 Clay St. (G)
Laxon, H.L., 2523 Western (G)
Lewis, R.E., 1324 High St. (Hdq)
Lindsey, Fred C., 1209 Fillmore (MG)
Losey, Karl, 1190 Fillmore (G)
Lynch, Chas., 1126 Oakland (D)
Oldham, G.T., RFD 1 (D)
Pressman, Chas., 506 Kansas (E) (L)
Souders, 110 W. 17th St. (I)
Swogger, Glenn, 3155 W. 15th (L)
Taylor, W.J., 2032 Burman Court
Wallace, Lew H., 521 Washburn (E)

TOWANDA
Priest, L.C. (D)

TROY
Clary, Charles I. (K)
Dannevik, John M., RFD 3 (K)
Molloy, T.B. (K)
Noyes, Robert F. (K)
Sallee, Emmett, RFD 1 (K)
Strong, H.D. (K)

ULYSSES
Bass, Chas. A. (A)
Sullivan, J.P. (Sup)

VALENCIA — RFD Silver Lake
Beal, Harlan E. (D)

VALLEY CENTER
Kesler, Fred (Amb)

VESPER
Anderson, Harry J. (M)

VICTORIA
Rajewski, Joseph (K)
Romme, Peter J. (L)

WAKEENEY
Klink, Frank (M)
Lamle, Paul O., Box 264 (M)
Schemm, John, RFD 2 (MG)

WALDO
Luder, J.K. (Hdq)

WALTON
McClure, Lester R. (Hdq)

WAMEGO
Knoebber, Frank H., 615 Vine (L)

WASHINGTON
Elder, Glenn (M)
Soller, W.A. (M)

WATERVILLE
Fisher, Wm. C. (M)
Winkenwader, F.A., RFD 2, Box 108 (L)

WATHENA
Behler, Simon, RFD 2 (K)
Boeh, R.M., RFD 3 (K)
Burns, George, RFD 3 (K)
Doro, Henry, RFD 3 (K)
Foley, Emmett H. (K)
Kasselhut, Robert, RFD 3 (K)
Marolf, George, RFD 3 (K)
Sigrist, Henry, RFD 1 (K)

WAVERLY
Bruner, E.R. (Hdq)
Frank, M.E., P.O. Box 134 (D)
Maine, Samuel A., RFD 1 (K)
Shaeffer, Logan B., RFD 1 (G)

WEIR
Hartman, Wm. D., Box 243 (L)

WELLINGTON
McConnell, Harry, 818 W. 18th (D)
Seal, Pleas A. (D)
Stephens, Chas. F., 1106 North C (H)
Voshell, Milo (K)

WELLS
Salsbery, Jasper C. (G)

WESTMORELAND
Mayer, Albert E. (D)

KANSAS *(continued)*
WICHITA
Alexander, A.A., Rt. 1, Box 392 (MG)
Baker, Albert L., 1847 N. Broadway (F)
Bennett, O.N., 307 N. Edwards (F)
Blume, Herman, 159 Circle Drive (B)
Brennan, S.C., 1822 N. Harvard (F)
Brew, Harry, 1014 S. Waco (I)
Brolund, Sam, 1480 Coolidge (Hdq)
Brown, Jerry I., 123 N. Estelle (Hdq)
Brownback, Lester C., 216 E. Waterman (Med)
Capron, Floyd, Pacific Hotel
Clark, Irvin R., 347 S. Erie (F)
Coats, Chas. M., 433 N. Quentin (Hdq)
Dodson, W. Frank, 455 S. Vassar (Hdq)
Eck, Ray B., 436 S. Clifton (D)
Edwards, Clay D., 2100 S. Terrace Dr. (Sup)
Field, Fred M., 1824 Parker (H)
Gillen, Harry, 536 S. Market (MG)
Hallgrimson, S., 2102 N. Broadway (L)
Hasty, Robert R., 625 First Nat'l Bank Bldg. (E)
Hiatt, Harry, 514 S. Main (Hdq)
Hotze, Alf. L., 734 S. Gordon (Sup)
Johnson, Albert A., 1107 N. Broadway (F)
Jones, R.B., 2501 Lulu (G)
Kaiser, Lester S., 1330 S. Clifton (H)
Knauss, John G., 1815 E. Lewis (D)
Kinkead, George, 2202-1/2 E. Douglas (A)
Kirby, Wm. M., RFD 6 (F)
Loman, F.A. (Jack), 205 N. Rutan (D)
Lowe, Claude, 1817 Ida (Hdq)
Maranville, Ness J., 237 S. Old Manor Rd. (F)
Marbinger, 522 Mathewson (D)
McClellan, 1440 E. 37th (SG)
McDonald, A.E., 312 New York (I)
McGinn, J.J., 225 S. Vine (E)
Middleton, C.E., 545 Everett (C)
Morton, P.M., 4347 E. Douglas (Amb)
Murphy, O.J., 3040 W. Central (H)
Mogle, Gayle, 1414 N. Emporia (Amb)
Osborne, Geo. W., 1121 S. Pershing (F)
Plagens, Otto, RFD 5 (M)
Postlewaithe, L., 1452 N. Waco (A)
Reed, Elmer, 2239 N. Market (A)
Rieniets, H.E., 640 S. Spruce (Hdq)
Salthouse, John, 4003 E. English (G)
Schoeppel, Adam J., 821 Litchfield (F)
Schwyart, H.E., 3923 Maple (C)
Shelly, Walter, 436 S. Lorraine (B)

Slagel, L.H., 418 E. English (E)
Slaybaugh, Floyd F., 4125 Menlo Dr. (D)
Smith, Dr. Charley, 322 S. Vassar (MG)
Smith, L.P., 738 Ida (D)
Snowhill, J.P., 411 S. Hydraulic (M)
Stuck, F.A., 639 S. Green (Amb)
Taylor, Herbert R., 3631 Litchfield (Hdq)
Telander, Arthur A., 3035 S. Sayles (C)
Tierney, Mike, 224 N. Exposition (F)
Tweed, J.H., 1811 N. Market (L)
Vandenburg, W.H., 1730 E. Kellogg (G)
Wald, O.E., 1030 S. Main (Hdq)
Wallis, H.N. 3402 E. Elm (Hdq)
Warne, Roy, 3730 S. Broadway (E)
Weaver, Jas. M., 1802 Parker (E)
Weaver, Walter H., 13345 N. West St. (Sup)
Wingate, Chas. R., 1027 Perry (L)
Wolf, Milton, 3406 W. 2nd (D)
WILLIAMSBURG
Sweetwood, Louis S. (Hdq)
WILSEY
Hudson, J.L. (Hdq)
WILSON
Kejr, John (Hdq)
WINFIELD
Beltz, David F., 801 E. 18th (L)
Howell, Dave M., 116 E. 11th (Amb)
Peterson, L.A., Box 154 (Med)
Shaw, J. Eldon, 1321 E. 8th (C)
Wilcox, Paul K., 1321 Hockney (Amb)
WINIFRED
Wanklyn, Albert L. (L)
WINONA
Ludlow, Roy A. (D)
WRIGHT
Buell, Ralph D. (F)
YATES CENTER
Beine, Wesley A., RFD 2 (Med)
Criswell, Roy (Amb)
Green, Chas. C. (C)
Robson, A.A., 900 E. Kansas (L)
Lauber, Emil, 113 E. Butler (L)
ZURICH
Gagnon, Francis D. (MG)

KENTUCKY
HAMPTON
Robinson, Byron H. (M)
LOUISVILLE
Jennings, Chas. R., 3185 Lexington Road (K)

MASSACHUSETTS
BINGHAM CENTER
  Harwood, Ralph W., 521 Main (B)
GLOUSTER
  Mooring, S.W. (Med)
NEWTON UPBER FALLS
  Connors, E.M., 12 William (A)
NORTH ADAMS
  LaBonte, Serine, 352 W. Shaft Road (Sup)

MICHIGAN
BERRIEN CENTER
  Hudson, William C. (K)
DETROIT
  Hewitt, James S., 1117 Book Bldg. (I)
GRAND RAPIDS
  Toenjes, Walter, RFD 5 (Hdq)
LANSING
  Carpenter, W.S., 750 E. Main (Fld)
PONTIAC
  Furlong, Harold A., 207 Navajo Road (M)
VAN DYKE
  Coggins, Geo A., 22718 Curie (A)

MINNESOTA
ATWATER
  Nelson, Elmer J., RFD 2 (L)
AUSTIN
  Meany, Dr. Francis P., Austin St. Bk.
    Bldg. (Med)
BELVIEW
  Johnson, Alfred, Rt. 1, Box 163 (C)
BUFFALO LAKE
  Dobberstein, Henry (K)
DULUTH
  Mickelson, C.J., 807 N. 57th Ave. W (C)
FERGUS FALLS
  Oyen, John, 219 Vernon Ave. E. (D)
FRAZEE
  Baumgart, Louis, RFD 1 (D)
HANCOCK
  Swanson, Fred R., Box 136 (K)
HAYWARD
  Nelson, Samuel L., RFD 1 (E)
HOPKINS
  Haskins, Elmer J., 237 13th Ave. N. (K)
KENT
  Krattenmaker, Louis P. (F)
KIMBALL
  Wilsanen, Kalle H., RFD 2 (C)

MINNEAPOLIS
  Anderson, Carl A., 4724 Blaisdell Ave. (M)
  Christenson, Wm. E., 3102 Logan Ave.
    N. (A)
  Halvorson, H.A., 5026 31st Ave., S. (B)
  Wycoff, Sydney V., 2606 Monroe St. (K)
MORRIS
  Henselin, Wm. H. (H)
PAYNESVILLE
  Lewerenz, Carl H. (E)
RED LAKE FALLS
  Karasiewicz, A.C., Box 421 (L)
REDTOP
  Rasmussen, Rockwell (L)
RENVILLE
  Danielson, Thore (F)
RUTLEDGE
  Anderson, Emil F. (G)
SOLVAY
  May, Arthur (D)
ST. PAUL
  Kopp, Burton G., 727 Wilson Ave. (B)
  Quast, Edward J., 389 Maple (B)
STRANDQUIST
  Anderson, Leroy (G)
THIEF RIVER FALLS
  Joringdale, Richard J., 327 Kendall Ave.,
    N. (L)
WEST BROOK
  Albertson, Clarence A. (I)

MISSOURI
AGENCY
  Farris, Carl H., RFD 1 (Sup)
BRUNSWICK
  Verhelst, Ben (L)
BUCKNER
  Reppert, Vernon M. (Hdq)
CARL JUNCTION
  Graves, Colver C., Box 150 (B)
CARUTHERSVILLE
  May, Harry C., Box 44 (K)
CHILLICOTHE
  Gunby, Fred W., 915 Walnut St. (D)
COLUMBIA
  Jones, C.C., 904 Virginia (D)
DE SOTO
  Nees, George R. (Amb)
DIXSON
  Cushing, John B., RFD 1 (C)
DREXEL
  Courtney, Joe J. (D)
  Hewitt, Morris E., RFD 1 (D)
  Lozar, Andrew A., Box 16 (H)

MISSOURI *(continued)*

ELDORADO SPRINGS
Keele, Everett (K)
FISK
Sisco, Granville E. (H)
FULTON
Van Sant, Thos. H., 834 Court (F)
GALENA
Randolph, Vance (F)
HANNIBAL
Russell, Frank T., City Bldg. (A)
HUNTER
Crump, C.K. (D)
HUNTSVILLE
McDowell, Hiram J., RFD 3 (H)
INDEPENDENCE
Glass, W.E., 2100 Scott (I)
ISHMAEL
Pratt, Carac, RFD 1 (H)
JOPLIN
Usher, Martin L., 2521 Wall (Hdq)
KANSAS CITY
Arnall, Glenn E., 6009 E. 13th (D)
Black, John W., 416 E. 70th (K)
Boolkin, Morris, 5137 Euclid (Hdq)
Boyle, P.A., 4312 Flora (C)
Bradley, John, 1032 Penn (E)
Britton, William, 3607 College (Hdq)
Brown, Osborn L., 3421 Michigan Ave. (B)
Burg, T. Stanley, 3418 Gillham Road (A)
Burns, F.G., 1323 E. 75th St. (Sup)
Calhoun, Emil, 5433 Highland (Med)
Deming, Homer, 601 E. 72nd St. (L)
Duncan, Arthur F., The Star (Amb)
Ebert, William, 4229 Tracy Ave. (B)
Funk, R.E., 4828 E. 7th St. (K)
Giese, Oscar L., 2038 E. Gregory (Sup)
Gray, Dr. G. Chas., 3600 Walnut St. (Fld)
Hall, Thos. N., 5443 Highland (C)
Harrouff, Earl R., 3921 Roanoke Rd. (M)
Hauber, Anthony W., 1201 W. 40th (A)
Holloman, John P., 2712 E. 33rd (H)
Houlihan, Martin J., 4127 Roanoke Road (C)
Hundley, R.A., 2931 Victor (F)
Leedy, Harold G., Fed. Reserve Bank (Hdq)
LeGrand, Lewis W., 6401 E. 15th Ter. (M)
McGrath, T.C., 812 Romany Road (A)
Milgram, David D., 441 W. 67th Ter. (Hdq)
Nuccio, Paul, 3424 Lexington (A)
Paulson, C.H., 2201 Meyer Blvd. (M)

Pennock, L.A., 7037 Montgall (Hdq)
Quinn, Peter J., 1032 Penn (Hdq)
Rinkel, Dr. Herbert J., 7300 Madison (Bd)
Risley, W.H., 2629 Chestnut (F)
Rooney, Wm. J., 712 W. 37th (F)
Schmidt, Chas. L., 1020 W. 41st (A)
Shivner, Eddie, 2553 Chelsa (B)
Spidel, W.E., 3746 Garfield (F)
Stein, L.F., 441 W. 60th Ter. (M)

Thompson, A.R., 3126 Mersington (Hdq)
Whitney, Oliver, 1833 Lister (K)
Wilson, C.E., 703 W. 38th (Med)
Witt, W.S., 3554 Genesee (D)
Woodhouse, J.R., 3422 Holmes (Hdq)
NORTH KANSAS CITY
Crockett, Clyde, 1000 E. 21st Ave. (H)
Farrell, E.W., 812 E. 24th Ave. (Hdq)
MANSFIELD
Lichty, L.D. (Sup)
MARSHALL
Reade, Roy, 1051 S. English (A)
NEVADA
Smith, L.C., 112 N. Tucker (Hdq)
NORBORNE
Gronniger, John L. (Hdq)
PATTONBURG
Davenport, Thomas B., RFD 1 (I)
PARKVILLE
Opperman, M.D., RFD 2 (Sup)
ROCKVILLE
Wood, John E., Box 51 (B)
ST. JOSEPH
Armour, Jas. W., 1221 No. 2nd (MG)
Thomas, G.B., 2815 Doniphan (D)
ST. LOUIS
Colwell, Harry L., 7571 Hoover Ave. (C)
Hulen, Ruby M., Fed. Bldg., 12th and Mkt. (A)
Manning, Frank B., 7338 Ahern Ave. (Hdq)
Ryan, Ray D., 4401 Forest Park (Hdq)
SALEM
Moser, Harry M. (G)
SARCOXIE
York, Dr. W.B. (Med)
SPRINGFIELD
Anderson, John J., 1618 S. Jefferson (D)
Costello, P.R. (Dick), 804 S. Florence (G)
SUMMERSVILLE
Bilbrey, Wade C., RFD 3 (A)
UNION STAR
Johnson, Randall A. (L)

MISSOURI *(continued)*
UNIVERSITY CITY
  Miller, Herbert H., 7336 Forsythe Blvd., Apt. 304 (G)
  Oliphant, Harry F., 6818 Washington St. (Sup)
WEBSTER GROVE
  Webster, Thomas W., 431 Yorkshire (L)

MONTANA
BILLINGS
  Maxwell, Dr. A.C., P.O. Box 462 (Med)
BOZEMAN
  Koopman, Leo H., Box 84 (F)
HELENA
  Parker, Ernest, Box 1711 Cadestral Eng. Ser. (C)
THOMPSON FALLS
  Matson, Andrew O. (K)

NEBRASKA
BARNSTON
  Ostendorf, Henry (Hdq)
FAIRBURY
  Washburn, C.H., 902 G St. (E)
FRANKLIN
  Wilsman, Earl M. (F)
HASTINGS
  Hayes, H.P., 841 N. Colorado Ave. (Hdq)
LINCOLN
  Cole, H.C., 1530 Cheyenne (Med)
  Lloyd, V.B., 1403 E. St. (F)
  Pentico, Lester C., 3879 Normal Blvd. (F)
MADRID
  Huber, Paul N. (H)
OMAHA
  Giger, Paul A., 4723 N. 30th (Med)
RED CLOUD
  Doering, Geo. F. (D)
VERDIGRE
  Pavelka, Vaclav, RFD 1 (Med)
WAKEFIELD
  Salley, O.D. (Hdq)
WOOD RIVER
  Shipps, Leo (Sup)

NEVADA
CARLIN
  Hand, Howard E. (D)
WINNEMUCCA
  Hamilton, John A. (Hdq)
YEARINGTON
  Lewin, Leo L. (K)

NEW JERSEY
NEWARK
  Martin, F.E., 725 High, Apt. 103 (E)
WEST NEW YORK
  Fenster, Joseph, 505 13th St. (F)

NEW MEXICO
ALBUQUERQUE
  Zurcher, Frank, 805 Loma Vista Dr. (Hdq)
PARK VIEW
  Martinez, Fidel F. (MG)

NEW YORK
BRIARCLIFF MANOR
  Christoph, Charles, Box 108, Route 1 (L)
GARDEN CITY, L.I.
  Fitzgerald (Mother) Mrs. L.K., 24 Franklin Court

OHIO
CLEVELAND
  Portman, Milton C., 600 Hicox Bldg. (E)
  Reese, T.M., 1825 E. 18th St. (L)
  Schlink, Dr. H.A., 208 Euclid (Med)
DAYTON
  Dorfmeier, Virgil Z., 814-820 Gas & Elec. Bldg. (I)
  Sheppard, Morton B., 901 Harvard Blvd. (D)
FINDLAY
  Hanna, Myron, 116 S. Main (Med)
TIPP CITY
  Davis, Larkin E., RFD 2 (D)

OKLAHOMA
CALUMET
  Moberly, Claude (K)
CARNEGIE
  Law, C.G., (Hdq)
COVINGTON
  Voigt, Paul A. (C)
GARBER
  Voigt, J.H., Box 492 (B)
CHICKASHA
  Frye, Norman F., 414 Chickasha (F)
HENRYETTA
  Abrams, R.F., 411 W. Gentry (F)
HOMINY
  Popkins, J.R. (Bd)
MUSKOGEE
  Towery, Fred J., 911 Fremant (Hdq)
NORMAN
  Wallace, J.B., 627 Jenkins (D)

OKLAHOMA *(continued)*
OKLAHOMA CITY
  Brown, L.H., 1213 Belford Ave. (C)
  McNally, Martin V., 1613 E. Park (A)
PAULS VALLEY
  Harvey, Frank (MG)
PONCA CITY
  Wollard, Lester L., 929 N. 3rd St. (B)
SELMAN
  Hopkins, Joseph J. (H)
TULSA
  Doughman, Claude L., 4630 S. Colum-
    bia (Hdq)
  O'Hara, Owen A., 3716 S. Union Place (F)
  Macon, R.H., 1336 S. Bermingham (Hdq)
  McLean, Jas. B., Rt. 5, Box 547 (H)
  Sharp, John E., 220 W. 19th St. (L)
VINITA
  Reed, Willis C., 322 W. Canadian (Med)
WAKITA
  Bailey, Frank (Sup)

OREGON
ASHLAND
  Karnes, Anthony E., 505 Fairview (MG)
  CORVALLIS
  Laslett, Herbert R., State College (Hdq)
EAGLE CREEK
  Wood, Frank M., Rt. 1 (D)
EUGENE
  Payne, Lloyd A., 245 E. Broadway (A)
FOREST GROVE
  Piatt, Wm. P., 118 C St., N. (Sup)
GRESHAM
  Hildebrand, Chas. (M)
MYRTLE POINT
  Bingham, Irwin, Box 35 (Sup)
PORTLAND
  Burnett, G.H. (Hal), 4055 S.E. Stark
    (Hdq)
  Homan, Ray, 1535 N.E. 55th Ave. (MG)
  Nelson, Clarence R., 109 N.W. 20th (M)
SUBLIMITY
  Hitchcock, Stanley S. (Bd)

PENNSYLVANIA
ALLENTOWN
  Young, Roy N., 2223 Allen St. (Hdq)
GROVE CITY
  Williams, 817 Stewart Ave. (K)
HARRISBURG
  Metzger, Leon D., 107 Hillside Road (D)

PHILADELPHIA
  Blackington, Geo W., 319 W. Chelten
    Ave. (Fld)

SOUTH CAROLINA
SUMMERVILLE
  Mitts, H.L., Squirrel Inn (A)

SOUTH DAKOTA
BROOKINGS
  Miller, Ward L., 921 Fifth St. (M)
FREDERICK
  Manu, Emil N. (D)
LEMMON
  Sinclair, Harold, Golden Rule Bldg. (Hdq)
PINE RIDGE
  Cottier, Eddie (I)
WATERTOWN
  King, Charles S., 319 9th St., N.W. (Hdq)

TEXAS
AMARILLO
  Sapp, P.F., 805 Oliver-Eakle Bldg. (MG)
ARANSAS PASS
  Peltier, Syrial (H)
AUSTIN
  Lockwood, J.W., U. of Texas (C)
BORGER
  Lantron, E.L., 907 S. Main (Hdq)
CORPUS CHRISTI
  Patty, L.L., 321 Atlantic (G)
  Shoop, A.L., 1346 Logan Ave. (D)
GOOSE CREEK
  Nelson, R.W., 114 W. Lobit St. (Bd)
MIDLAND
  Hefner, A.C. Scharbauer Hotel (Bd)
PAMPA
  Hunt, J. Frank, 1138 N. Russell (Hdq)
WICHITA FALLS
  Younger, James G., 2008 9th St. (Bd)

UTAH
SALT LAKE CITY
  Wood, Charles, 1950 S. 5th (Hdq)

VIRGINIA
ARLINGTON
  Hoover, Elmer J., 4622 N. 14th St. (Hdq)
KECOUGHTAN
  Meeker, George, Box 400 (C)

WASHINGTON

BREMERTON
Hull, W.E., Rt. 2, Box 413-A (E)
ESPANOLA
Dundeen, Leonard G. (Sup)
LACENTER
Wulf, Alfred, Route 1, Box 78 (H)
SEATTLE
Ferguson, Sam H., 2420 Monte Vista
Place (Med)
SPOKANE
Aydelotte, Alfred L., E. 303 31st Ave. (Bd)
WARDEN
Trautman, Jacob (Bd)
TACOMA
McAuley, M.E., 4638 S. Yakima St. (Bd)

WEST VIRGINIA

ALDERSON
Eades, Carl G., Box 185 (F)
CLARKSBURG
Oberg, John A. (I)
CLAYTON
Ballenger, Kyle L. (MG)

WISCONSIN

ABRAMS
Steinkraus, Otto G., RFD 1 (MG)
APPLETON
Bosch, Paul, RFD 4 (MG)
Liethen, John H., 612 W. College Ave.
(Sup)
Reetz, Wm., 1107 W. Oklahoma St. (E)
ALMOND
Keenlance, Albert H., RFD 1 (C)
ASHLAND
Eriksen, Karl A., 310 6th Ave., W. (G)
BOYD
Bourget, Lawrence, RFD 1 (F)
CLEAR LAKE
Olson, Eddie (M)
COLBY
Frome, Edwin L. (C)
COLUMBUS
Plats, Norton S., 332 Campbell (G)
CROSS PLAINS
Faust, Englebert (K)
CUDAHY
Zdunek, John, 3927 E. Plankington Ave.
(E)
CUMBERLAND
Shields, Edward J., RFD 1 (F)

DELAVEN
Flood, Leo (L)
Huntress, Harold, RFD 2 (K)
EAU CLAIRE
Moore, Robert L., 1205 State St. (C)
ELKHORN
Welkos, Irving G. (MG)
Wilcox, Alice (A)
ELROY
Preuss, Arthur R., RFD 2 (L)
FON DU LAC
Kaufman, Andrew C., 196 Haas Pl. (F)
Smith, Ewald, RFD 3 (L)
FORT ATKANSON
Urban, Carl, 421 N. High (E)
FREMONT
Bauer, Henry F. (D)
GENOA CITY
Diegnan, Jas. (D)
Long, Chas. B. (E)
GREENWOOD
Fravert, Otto H., RFD 2, Box 20 (E)
HANCOCK
Nelson, John, RFD 1 (MG)
HILBERT
Mullenbach, Michael (I)
HUDSON
Peterson, P.A., 1209 7th St. (B)
INDEPENDENCE
Tubbs, Lon F. (L)
JEFFERSON
Schroeder, George, RFD 3 (I)
JUNEAU
Seegert, Emil C., RFD 3 (C)
LaCROSSE
Hansen, Herman, 222 S. 19th St. (C)
Strittmater, W., 1530 Jackson (M)
Wuensch, Lawrence, 1323 Farman St.
(M)
LAKE MILLS
Korth, Edwin R., 207 College St. (E)
LOHRVILLE
Bergholz, Arthur G. (K)
MADISON
Shaunessey, Joseph J., 414 W. Laton (H)
MARATHON
Seubert, August, RFD 1 (H)
MARATHON CITY
Witberler, Otto, RFD 2 (H)
MENASHA
Voissem, George (K)
MENOMINEE FALLS
Gehlert, Leroy (I)

WISCONSIN *(continued)*
MERRILL
Maas, Herbert G., 2100 River St. (G)
MILWAUKEE
Fenner, Wm. C., 2475-A W. Keefe Ave. (F)
SO. MILWAUKEE
Thiede, Wm. F., 914 Manitoba Ave. (M)
MUKWONAGO
Dahms, John, 223 Grand Ave. (B)
NEENAH
Austin, Harvey F., 121 Second St. (B)
Austin, Myron J., 121 Second St. (B)
NEKOOSA
Belgert, Gustave C., 740 Point Basse Ave. (D)
NEW AUBURN
Horn, Carl C. (E)
Olson, Edward L., RFD 2 (D)
O'Rourke, Arthur E., RFD 4 (I)
NEW LONDON
Ploetz, Rudolph R. (D)
NORWALK
Kruk, Joseph (B)
OCONOMOWOC
Miller, Arthur G., RFD 2 (L)
OCONTO
Ravey, Herman G., 1204 Superior Ave. (B)
OMRO
Kleinschmidt, Geo. A., RFD 3 (I)
OSHKOSH
Hart, James, RFD 3, Box 1 (B)
Weber, Kantius, 904 8th St. (M)
PALMYRA
Brigham, Merle (A)
PARK FALLS
Lucas, Mike (B)
PESHTIGO
Kasten, Arthur C., Gen. Del. (H)
RIDGEWAY
Leary, Leo F. (I)
ROBERTS
Schwalen, Henry T., RFD 1 (H)

SHARON
Jacobi, Lee (L)
LaBundy, Ernest H. (L)
SHEBOYGAN
Den Boer, Frank, 115 Lincoln Ave. (M)
SHEBOYGAN FALLS
Roska, Herbert C., 105 Pine St. (M)
SHIOCTON
Berendts, Herman A., RFD 1 (K)
SOLDIERS GROVE
Swiggum, Melvin A., RFD 2 (K)
STRATFORD
Spencer, John (H)
STRUM
Peterson, Edwin H. (F)
TROY CENTER
Branfort, A.C. (A)
VAN DYNE
Gilbertson, E.M., RFD 1 (F)
WATERTON
Ebert, Arthur, 311 Elizabeth St. (C)
Schumacher, Geo. C., 215 3rd St. (C)
WEST ALLIS
Meyer, Roman A., 1530 S. 60th (L)
WINNECONME
Ryan, Samuel M., Main St. (F)

WYOMING
TORRINGTON
Boundurant, Henry B., 115 E. 23rd Ave. (F)

DISTRICT OF COLUMBIA
WASHINGTON
Dickason, W.E., 1517 Oats, N.E. (C)
English, Col. Geo. H. Hay-Adams House (Fld)

CANADA
DISLEY, SASK.
Howell, Thos. B. (M)

WOES OF A K.P.

Yes, they took me in the army,
  Gave me shoes and uniform,
Made a kitchen soldier of me,
  Far from where the battles storm.
I ain't got no gun or bayonet,
  Never seen a cannon yet —
All I do is wipe the dishes,
  Do you wonder that I fret?

Yes, I wipe, wipe, wipe.
Gee! The beggars keep us workin'
  half the night,
An' there ain't no blood and thunder,
'Ceptin' when you make a blunder.
Lord! I wish I had a gun, so's I
  could fight.

All the blessed, livin' daytime
  On a hard and narrow seat,
We just sit and wipe our dishes
  An' it's awful in the heat.
While the sun beats down like fury,
  While the dust is everywhere,
We just sit and wipe our dishes,
  Prayin' for a breath of air.

We just wipe, wipe, wipe.
Gee! The beggars keep us working
  half the night,
  And they laugh at us and jeer us,
  For no enemy ain't near us.
Lord, I wish I had a gun so's I could
  fight.

We just sit and wipe the dishes,
  Scrub the tables, sweep the floor,
Serve the beans, the spuds and coffee,
  Till the beggars eat no more.
Then we start our work all over
  For our job is never done,
Till the Mess Hall's once more shinin',
And the evenin' sun is gone.

But we wipe, wipe, wipe,
Gee! The beggars keep us workin'
  half the night.
  Yep, we're in the Kitchen Police.
  If you ask us, why, it's fierce.
Lord, I wish I had a gun so's I could
  fight.

For we'll stay here tho' it's over
  And the boys come marchin' back,
Tellin' how they licked the Germans,
  How they gave Wilhelm the sack,
And even then they'll keep us —
  Lettin' out those we let in —
Then they'll send us back to home folks
  Who will greet us with a grin.

For we just wiped, wiped, wiped.
No, we didn't cross no ocean in a boat,
  And we didn't see no fightin'
  We were too damn busy, wipin'.
Do you wonder that I think I am the
  goat?

  — Private Harvey E. Regg,
  Base Hospital, Det. Med. Dept.,
  Camp Pike, Arkansas

ANSWER TO THE
"WOES OF A K.P."

By his mother, Mrs. O.W. Reeg, Altus, Okla.

I am thinking today of a dear K.P.
*   Far away at Camp Pike,*
And I know that you will think of me
*   As you the dishes wipe.*

I know you are disappointed
*   To be kept there in the grind,*
While your friends cross over the
*   ocean*
*   And you were left behind.*

All honor to the boys who fought,
*   All honor to the men*
Who went with the stars and stripes
*   to France*
*   To bring us Peace again.*

But we know that there were many
*   who longed to go*
*   And were never given a chance*
To help the Allies down the foe
*   And gain freedom again for France.*

For they cannot all be heroes
*   With crosses on their breast,*
But we honor every one of them
*   Who did their level best.*

And you are doing your duty
*   For dear old Uncle Sam,*
Tho' you've never seen a battle
*   As have others of our land.*

And we'll greet you just as proudly
*   When you come marching back*
As if you'd been there with them
*   When they gave "Wilhelm the*
*   sack."*

Your mother knows just how you feel
*   As you work from dawn till night.*
You wish that you could have gone
*   to France*
*   And been in the thick of the fight.*

She knows just all about it,
*   She's been a K.P. all her life;*
But that was just her duty,
*   As a mother and a wife.*

We think we're not much honored,
*   But when all is said and done,*
If it were not for those in the kitchens,
*   They could never have licked the*
*   Hun.*

So you see when accounts are
*   settled*
*   And every one given their due,*
In helping to win the great World War,
*   That one of them was you.*

30 A General View of Camp Funston, Ks. Olson Photo

When my dad, George W. Gardner, went to Camp Funston, they assigned him to the Awkward Squad, which were men who could not keep time to music. One thing about my dad: he never complained any time while he was in service.

CAMP FUNSTON MEMORIAL.
ERECTED BY THE BOYS WHO TRAINED
THERE, FOR THE WORLD WAR.

Gen. View. Camp Funstan, Kans.

Kansas Bldg. Camp Funstan Kans.

G.W. Gardner

Left: Sgt. Thompson, Sgt. Gardner, Sgt. King, Sgt. Erickson.

When the 89th Division, 353rd Infantry, left Camp Funston, Lt. Ward Gardner was commander. My brother, Kenneth Ward Gardner, was named after him. All the division was headed for New York City and then to Europe. While in New York, they wanted to see some of the sights, and all ran toward the train depot. Lt. Ward Gardner tried to stop them, for there in the depot were all the top brass. That would have been quite a feeling. Then they all marched back to the base.

PERSONNEL OF THE 353rd INFANTRY

September 5, 1917, has been set as the birthday of the 353rd Infantry, 89th Division. Colonel Reeves and many of the officers were on the ground several days earlier, but not until September 5 did the "first five per cent" of the Regiment's enlisted personnel arrive in the unit area at Camp Funston. Five months lacking one day since the declaration of war between the United States and Germany on April 6, 1917, had been spent in preparation of this mere beginning of the mobilization and organization of man power for the nation's part in the World War. The cantonment had been built, the equipment supplied, officers trained. Now the Selective Service Law was in operation. And the "Rookies," veterans of the future, were actually born into the service. Only those who have left civil occupations and homes for the camp and field can ever appreciate the change which this transition brings into the lives of men. It is little wonder that the 5th of each succeeding month grew in significance for every man in the 353rd Infantry.

The personnel of the Regiment, as of the entire National Army, came from three sources: the Regular Army, the Officers' Reserve Corps, and the citizenship of the country between the ages of twenty-one and thirty-one years. The initial personnel of the 353rd Infantry follows: From the Regular Army; Col. James H. Reeves, Lieut. Col. Frank B. Hawkins, Maj. Jans E. Stedge, Maj. W.F.C. Jepson, and thirty-four non-commissioned officers. From the Officers' Reserve Corps: eighty-four officers (from the 5th Company, 14th Provisional Training Regiment at Fort Riley). From the State of Kansas under the operation of the Selective Service Law: three hundred twenty-three enlisted men on September 5; one hundred eighty on October 5th — a total of two thousand nine hundred seventy-four Kansas men. From these initial increments of National Army men the Regiment received its name, "The All-Kansas Regiment."

Like all National Army Regiments the 353rd Infantry was called upon to transfer men to other organizations and to receive replacements from later drafts. These transfers were made to the Engineers' Corps, to the Headquarters Battalion of the A.E.F., to the Aviation Section of the Signal Corps, and various other branches of the service where men were immediately needed. The largest detachments were sent to the 35th Division and to the 4th Division. A.E.F. officers, too, were transferred to various organizations, and twenty-eight others from the 2nd training Camp at Fort Benjamin Harrison began their service in the Regiment in December, 1917.

These unsettled conditions in the personnel of the Regiment were trying to both officers and men. "Are we to be a depot outfit after all?" was a question of frequent recurrence. The final effect of the transfers is seen in this announcement of the Regimental Bulletin of April 11, 1918:

> "Each company will turn out on Friday afternoon at the parade for General Wood with six squads. Battalion Commanders will notify these Headquarters of the number of men needed in each company to make up this quota."

Timely assurance from the War Department saved the morale of the men. The Regimental Bulletin of February 19 had this announcement:

"From a letter received by the Division Commander from the War Department it is desired that all officers and men understand that there is no intention of breaking up National Army Divisions. All should co-operate most heartily for the benefit of the army as a whole."

Further assurance came on February 25th in the requirement of "indispensable lists." "All non-commissioned officers plus 5% of the remaining enlisted strength" were to be retained in each company. There were still enough when reduced to the lowest number to "carry on," and soon replacements began to appear. With new men came new hope of service over sea.

These replacements were as follows:

March 13, 1918,	350 men,	Camp Grant, Illinois. 161st Depot Brigade.
April 24, 1918,	300 men,	Camp Funston, Kansas. 164th Depot Brigade.
April 27, 1918,	143 men,	Camp Funston, Kansas. 164th Depot Brigade.
May 8, 1918,	2017 men,	Camp Funston, Kansas. 164th Depot Brigade.

The monthly return for May, 1918, made up at Camp Mills, N.Y., showed a total of three thousand five hundred two enlisted men and one hundred officers in the Regiment. The Medical Detachment, in addition, consisted of fifty-two men and eleven officers. The regiment was now practically up to war strength.

But changes in personnel must continue and were now accepted as part of the game. In the place of "indispensables" all became "expendibles." Nineteen lieutenants came to the Regiment in The Reynel Training area, France, from the A.E.F. candidates school. While all were rejoicing in a more complete line-up of officers for early duty at the front, several of the old officers were recalled to the United States as instructors.

These changes in personnel seemed at the time to be striking at the progress and efficiency of the organization. There's something in the association of men as "bunkies" that ties them together once for all. "I'm ready to go," said the transferred men, "but I should like to go with my old outfit." And the man who was left behind answered, "We're going to be filled up with strangers. I don't like it either." But it remained for the experience of campaigns to reveal the true value of replacements for renewed effectiveness. When the ranks had been thinned in the Lucey Sector, in the St. Mihiel Offensive, and in the Euvezin Sector, seven hundred eighty-one new men from the 86th Division found little difficulty in swinging into line with the veterans of previous campaigns. The new men were glad to give some of their extra shoes and equipment to the old men; and the old men free to give the new men the full benefit of their experience as fighters.

These replacements from the 86th Division were from various middle-western states — Illinois, Minnesota, Wisconsin, Nebraska and South Dakota mainly. The enlisted personnel of the Regiment remained approximately sixty per cent Kansas men throughout the entire period of service. The officers, however, represented every state in the union. And "The All Kansas Regiment" came to be the most typically middle-west regiment of the Middle-West Division.

More important than the numbers and source of this personnel were its qualifications for the task and its qualities of character, which accounts for its high service as a part of the A.E.F. The four officers and thirty-four non-commissioned officers of the Regular Army were to form the framework of the new organization. These men, especially Colonel Reeves, game to the Regiment its policies and standards of efficiency.

For twenty-nine years Colonel Reeves had seen continuous military service. His service included duty with troops, staff work, special duty with the Philippine Government, and long experience as a military attaché. This broad experience gave him a sympathetic understanding of men as well as military affairs, both essential to the building of a National Army regiment. Lieutenant Colonel Hawkins, second in command from the organization of the Regiment until the occupation of the Lucey Sector, had been in the service since the Spanish-American War. His experience at the Fort Slocum and Fort Logan Recruit Depots was especially valuable in the training of the new National Army men. Major Stedge enlisted as a private in 1894. He not only knew soldiering at first hand from the ranks to the commissioned grades, but even more important, Major Stedge impressed the new men in unmistakable and picturesque terms with the gravity of military service. He "nailed them to the cross" and at the same time strengthened their confidence in themselves. Major Jepson was with the Regiment only a few days when he was transferred to another organization.

More immediate than the influence of the Regular Army officers was the service of the non-commissioned personnel of the Regular Army. They spoke not of years but of "hitches" in the service. They understood guard mount exactly and knew the technique of the duty roster to the fraction of a minute even though its tours were longer in the National Army than they had ever known with the Regulars. They surprised the new Reserve Officers with their ready use of the third person and taught its practical value to the rookies. They were soldiers by profession and played the game in a manner worthy of the best traditions of the old army.

These officers and enlisted men of the Regular Army were a tried lot. Thorough training and actual experience gave them confidence in themselves and the record they had made, entitled them the confidence of the whole country. But there was a bit of apprehension about the future of the new officers and enlisted men who were to take part in the World War with so little training and even less experience. This apprehension was greatest in the minds of the officers and men themselves. True to American spirit, however, they balanced lack of confidence with determination and lack of experience with intensity of effort.

The Reserve Officers of the 353rd Infantry were men who responded to the call for volunteers under Section 54 of the National Defense Act, June, 1916. They were plain citizens who wished to serve their country to the fullest. Of the eighty-four who reported to Camp Funston for duty with the Regiment, fifteen had been engaged in business, eight had left study in colleges and universities, six resigned as teachers, and others came from such occupations as law, journalism, engineering, and medicine. Of these same men, three had had training in military schools, nine had seen service in the National Guard, ten had been in the Regular Army, and the rest were wholly inexperienced in military matters. In respect to the variety of their previous occupations and their military experience these men were representative of the Reserve Officers of the National Army generally.

These officers began their training at Fort Riley in May and received their commissions in August. Training Camp Bulletin No. 49 has some striking statements concerning the process. For example, "The schedule is based on a minimum day of ten hours." As a matter of fact, the day was not based on hours at all but upon the limit of human endurance. "All must forget rank," the bulletin continued, "and live and work on equal terms." Training began with a "hike"; by the end of the week company drill was in progress. By the sixth week range work was on with drill between platoon turns at firing. In spite of dust and heat, inoculations and vaccinations, the men stuck to the schedule. Occasionally the surgeons ruled out a candidate on physical disability, but no one "fell out." It was understood from the first that commissions would be granted on the basis of the survival of the fittest. General Sherman's epithet came to be freely applied to training camps as well as to war. The men, however, recognized in these strenuous conditions the peril of their country and did their best to help redeem a bad situation.

In this connection a word of recognition is due the officers of the Regular Army for the part they played in training the new officers. Capt. Levi G. Brown (later Lieutenant-Colonel Brown) commanded the 5th Company, 14th Provisional Training Regiment, in which the first officers assigned to the 353rd Infantry were trained. He appreciated fully the position of a candidate called from the ranks for the first time to take charge of a company. If a mix-up occurred because the commander forgot his command, or those commanded had no chance to execute *automatically,* the captain never scored until he saw the final solution of the situation. To avoid a bad situation was commendable; to save a bad situation was creditable. Regular Army officers held to their standards of efficiency but almost without exception they emphasized these standards as goals to be approached and not as ends immediately attainable.

Under this instruction the candidates from civilian life had by the 15th of August, as summed up by Colonel Rivers, the Camp Commander in his final message to the successful candidates in the Riding Hall at Fort Riley, "a slight knowledge of a good many things." His parting words were, "Remember it's up to you to justify your commissions." In this statement he revealed the secret of success to the new officers. They took the cue without hesitation. In camp the new officers studied while their men rested on the drill ground, attended battalion schools at night, crammed for special examinations — all this under threat of summons before the "benzine" board. Not by the acquirements of three months in the training camp did they succeed but by ceaseless effort throughout their entire service.

The third element in the personnel of the 353rd Infantry, the enlisted men, was, above all, typical of the population of the Middle West. A glance at any roster revealed almost every language. The following are specimens from Company "A": McClowsky, Christensen, Armigo, Lopriore, Biskoe, Van Dusen, England, Plov, Kirschbaum, Massier. While all nationalities were represented, few were of foreign birth; ancestry of the men of the 353rd infantry was usually stated in the Service Record, "American." Even more striking than the sound of their names was the appearance of the men themselves as they stood in line even for the first time. They were tall, broad-shouldered men with tan on their faces and blisters on their hands. They looked each other and their officers straight in the eyes with a guarantee of intelligence, sincerity, and loyalty that inspired confidence immediately. They needed only the precision and discipline of military drill to make of them soldiers fit for the arduous duties of the World War. As the historian of Company "G" observed,

"It was a cosmopolitan outfit that boarded the train at Camp Funston, May 26, 1918, and started on the 'Long, Long Trail.' They were Americans going to shatter the imperialistic aspirations of the Potsdam gang."

The enlisted men of the Regiment, like the Reserve Officers, represented all lines of civilian occupation. One hundred men taken in alphabetical order from the roster of Headquarters Company claimed thirty-nine different occupations. Twenty-seven of these were farmers, seven were miners; railroad men, salesmen, barbers, tailors, and others followed. This variety in experience fitted well into the needs of the new organizations. Company Commanders lost no time in investigating the ability of their men and soon had each one working at his highest efficiency. Carpenters completed the barracks, cooks went to the kitchens, barbers and tailors established their shops. No matter what the task (with the possible exception of bugling), there could be found in the Regiment a man equal to the occasion, already trained in the school of civilian service.

Very few had had any experience in military matters — and yet the list of non-commissioned officers picked from the new men numbered two hundred sixteen by October 1st. It was made clear at the outset that merit was to be the basis of promotion in the National Army. The response of the men to this challenge of duty and opportunity is seen in the fact that eighty-three enlisted men of the 353rd Infantry were sent to Officers' Training camps. The enlisted personnel did not, however, accept military service as a profession. It was the end to be attained, not the process of attaining the end, that called forth their utmost efforts. On the night of the 31st of October, just preceding the advance in the Meuse-Argonne Offensive, the 353rd Infantry was commended because there was not a single straggler, but when the call was made for re-enlistment at the time of demobilization not a man volunteered. The end of the war had been attained. The soldier's interest returned irresistibly to home and civilian occupation.

In brief, the personnel of the 353rd Infantry, both in its source and qualifications was typically American. Its elements were called together from peaceful pursuits, under pressure of one of the gravest emergencies that had ever occurred in the life of the Nation. The representatives of the Regular Army realized fully the task of building an organization to contend with the disciplined veterans of Europe. They were steadied in their part by thorough training and actual service under fire. The new officers and men accepted without reserve the call to service. They brought to the task the vigor and determination of the Middle-West. Finally, through all ranks and elements ran, with ever increasing power, the consciousness of obligation to the principles recognized throughout the world as American.

—

CONFIDENTIAL.   Washington, D.C., May 16, 1918.
Commanding General, 89th Division,
Camp Funston, Kansas.

Send troops now at your camp reported ready and equipped for over-sea service to Port of Embarkation, Hoboken, N.J. Arrange time of arrival and other details directly with the Commander of Port … Have inspections made to determine if Organizations and individuals are properly supplied with serviceable clothing, equipment and medical supplies. Report of result shall be made by telegram. Leave all alien enemies behind.

(Signed) — McCain.

In his endorsement, General Wood added, "Officers and enlisted men will be required to work without regard to hours in order to prepare organization for shipment." When this telegram was received, the Regiment was encamped at the target range five miles away. Most of the non-commissioned officers were on detached service. Of course, the exact date of entrainment was not given, but passenger cars were being spotted by the scores on the switch above Camp Funston. The Regiment must get ready on a few hours notice to move with the Division.

Orders came thick and fast, but directions were vague. "What are we to take?" was the first question. In a conference with Captain Piatt the following classification was received: "Light Baggage, Heavy Baggage, and Freight." The dividing line between the members of this classification varied with succeeding conferences. When the G.I. Cans had all been labeled and numbered as Heavy Baggage they were ordered shipped as Freight. In the meantime these same G.I. Cans had been filled with valuable baggage which could never go as Freight. The resulting confusion was sometimes embarrassing as well as inconvenient. For these G.I. Cans had been packed with forbidden articles, such as athletic equipment and officers' boots. When the boxes had been made, painted, stenciled, packed, measured, weighed and nailed up, the problem arose of "turning in" the surplus accumulation of many months. After it had all been turned in several times there was still Government property hanging on the walls, in the store rooms, and many other places that had bee carefully policed.

The main task these days was equipping the men. Truck loads were hauled out to the rifle range and truck loads were hauled back to be "turned in." The Supply Company insisted on receipts and Company Commanders signed with fear and trembling. Supply Sergeants were the busiest men in the Camp these days. They emptied barrack bags and "turned in" what they considered disallowed for over-seas service and substituted according to Equipment "C." Sizes ran odd as usual and when the men returned Supply Sergeants were the most unpopular men in the Regiment. But this was war, and "Orders were Orders."

Eight trains were allotted to the 353rd Infantry, approximately one train for two companies. Loading began on May 25th; strictest secrecy was enjoined upon all; under no consideration was any one to breathe the name of his organizations or the Camp where it had trained; no letters were to be mailed from the train. In spite of all these warnings and precautions, crowds were at the station to cheer the soldiers on their way, and when no one was looking some appreciative American girl would carefully collect all the out-going mail. The route ran through Kansas City, St. Louis, Frankfort, Cleveland, and Buffalo to Hoboken, New Jersey. This was the first trip across the country, and cities were doubly busy with the rush of war-time industry. "A man can afford to fight for a country like this," was the growing conviction as the train rolled on.

The climax of interest came in the trip down the Hudson from Hoboken to Long Island station. Here were the things all had heard about: the tallest building in the world; Brooklyn Bridge; war ships — the activity expressive of the life of the nation's greatest port.

TO BATTLE ON STRETCHER
"Big Bill" Refused To Let Just an Operation Stop Him.
Negro Soldiers Expected To See Their Colonel in Their First Fight and Made Him Proud He Defied Surgeons.

This story probably relates to William Hayward of Nebraska and New York, who went to the front in command of a New York negro regiment. He was born in Nebraska City, Neb., and practiced law there. He was chairman of the Republican state committee and later secretary of the Republican national committee. Shortly after he made his home in New York City he became an assistant district attorney. He managed successfully the campaign of Governor Whitman of that state, and was later named public service commissioner for New York City. He was personally very popular. When the war began, he gave up his law practice to take command of the negro regiment.

BY HERBERT COREY.

WITH THE AMERICANS IN FRANCE, Aug. 23— (By mail.)—There is a point in the procession of military rank at which the censor's curtain falls between the performancec and the public. Lieutenants may do gallant things and the story may be told. Sometimes captains may be mentioned. Less often majors win their need of recognition, but colonels are not to be named.

So this is just "Big Bill's" story. There are plenty of Big Bills in the American army, just as the army is full of "Fighting Fifteenths" and other fighting numbers. Every regiment that gets near enough to the German to put its hands on him immediately becomes a "fighting" something or other, and so far as I know they have all deserved it. The American material is no better than it has always been, but the American discipline is. The American youngsters are soldiers when they reach this side. Barely a touch of fire is needed to harden them.

KNEW HIS REGIMENT.

But that was not the case with "Big Bill's" regiment. He had organized that regiment himself, and daddied it and loved it. He knew almost every man in it, but he had not been given time to hammer it into perfected form. The regiment was rushed over to France after little more than a month's training on Long Island. Then it

was slammed right into the front line. If the men had been a bit skittish, one could not have blamed them. They had not had that intensive training which makes fighting men out of rookies. But if they were skittish, the Germans did not find it out. They held the line. So the regiment went along, getting used to its job. It had been four months in line when the counter offensive started July 18. The record is by no means a unique one, but it is a record to be proud of. Men who can stand that without getting trench stale are first rate fighting men.

But the colonel may have worried about it. Once when he was one of America's football heroes he had broken his ankle, and the break had returned to plague him. From time to time other things had happened to him, too, so that the surgeons sent him to a hospital. The colonel had protested:

"I won't go unless you promise to send for me if we put on a show," he said.

"SURE, BILL."

"Sure, Bill," said the surgeons. You know that easy assurance of a surgeon. "Sure, Bill," they said — just like that. Then they put him on the operating table and rearranged his anatomical plan to suit themselves. They figured that he'd be mighty near a perfect man when they got through. He was as weak as a kitten and wound up in bandages and had an ankle in splints when he heard the show had started. He called the head surgeon:

"I've got to go to my regiment," said he.

"Nonsense, Bill," said the head surgeon. "You're as leaky as a dory. If you stand up, you'll tear like a dishrag."

"Those boys of mine are going into battle," said the colonel. "Get out of my way."

So they picked up his stretcher and started him on his way. The surgeon said they just naturally had to have their minds clear for what was coming, and they could not if he was in the house. He got to his regiment at a time when it was moving about like quicksilver on a hot plate. The boche was reacting vigorously, and it was the regiment's job to be on the spot in readiness for each reaction. Between times the regiment found a chance to sort of whisk broom and tiptoe its way into the room where "Big Bill" lay on his stretcher.

"The boys, dey mighty proud to see you back wid us again, Kunnel," said Casey Jones, of New York, who is "Big Bill's" cook.

MOVED SEVEN TIMES.

Seven times in seven days regimental headquarters were moved. Each time the colonel moved with them on a stretcher. There was a wholly competent second in command, and the colonel did not interfere in any fashion. But the second in command wants it understood that this was "Big Bill's" battle.

"He made this regiment," said he, "and he made its spirit. I only carried out his plans as he would have me carry them out."

When the battle was over, the colonel was carried back to the hospital, still on his stretcher. Under his pillow was a slip of paper which had been handed him by the French general who commanded the division of which his regiment was a part. It was the list of the citations given to his men for gallantry in action.

HARD ON THE HUN TANKS
American Artillery Applies "Goulash Wagon" Tactics with Great Success.

WITH THE AMERICAN ARMY IN FRANCE, Sept. 12 (by mail). — In a certain division, they never get through telling about their artillery. They are proud of the artillery, and the artillery is proud of its work.

Down in Lorraine the artillery had a sport which turned out to be something better than a game when the division took its stand east of Reims. The artillerymen used to shoot at German "goulash wagons" and trucks coming down the roads behind the Lorraine lines. The Americans got quite expert at upsetting traffic as it rolled toward the front.

Near Reims the artillery found bigger game. It was tanks. Out in front of the positions held by the Allies were some low sandy hills over which the Germans sent their tanks to harass the American positions. When the first tank crawled over the brow of the hill, an artilleryman applying the "goulash wagon" tactics planted a shell squarely in the middle of the tank.

Meantime, other batteries got four more Hun tanks one by one as they crawled to a cross-road just behind the advanced German positions. The Germans were amazed at the accuracy of the fire, and found tanks a costly proposition when the better part of their fleet of more than twenty-five was damaged beyond use by the artillery, before the tanks could fire a shot.

OUR MEN LEARN QUICKLY
Nothing Educational Escapes Them, Doctor Jenkins Says

The American Is Always Looking for Short Cuts and Becomes Impatient When Asked to Follow Precedents.

By Burris A. Jenkins.

SOMEWHERE IN FRANCE, Sept. 12. — The American soldier is *sui generis,* of his own sort. He is like no other the world ever made. His composite blood, his new western environment, the character of his life and thought, have all combined to give him a different appearance and a different movement from any of the rest.

His step is lighter than others, or else he has that effect upon the imagination; which amounts to the same thing. He may not move faster, nor with more elasticity than some other troops, but he seems less tied to the earth, less to touch it in his tread. His movements, therefore, seem to proceed more from nerve than from muscle, although both are, of course, apparent. All this may be, to be sure, the biased interpretation of an overpartial mind; and yet others of other nationality have expressed themselves in the same strain.

COLLEGE GRADUATES FAST WORKERS.

The lieutenant of engineers told me at luncheon of a new record established by his outfit inlaying narrow gauge track. There was a record of some twelve thousand feet in twelve hours, which was cabled to President Wilson, and over which there was much to do. His men, he told me, had laid 14,200 feet in less than seven hours, and he beamed with pride. Most of his pick and shovel men were college graduates.

Then he told of a little Jew in his company, who had been a clerk in a railway office at home, drawing $95 a month. He was about to recommend the little man as a corporal, when the others began accusing the Hebrew of laziness and inefficiency. The lieutenant heard a few days later that the lad had fought the night before with an Irishman from 6 till 9:30 o'clock and were stopped by taps. It was 3-minute rounds, with a minute rest. Both men had worked the day before, all day, and both worked the next day as if nothing had happened, though they could barely see, their faces were raw beef and they had spat out most of their teeth. Needless to say, the Jew got his corporalship. The lieutenant saw to it, too, that both the Jew and the Irishman were put on kitchen patrol the next Sunday so they would not to appear at inspection.

AMERICANS NEVER GRUMBLE.

It is a pity that these high grade men are compelled to do hard labor, although they can do twice as much in a given time as any labor battalion that was ever enlisted. I am informed, however, that the condition has been remedied and the college men are rapidly being given positions of direction and leadership.

The defeat of this characteristic lies, perhaps, in an unwillingness for the hard work involved in this war. All war is labor, but this war more than any other. Four-fifths of the effort put forth in this great conflict is just labor, one-fifth fighting. It is in the running of factories back home, in the transportation, in the building of railways, docks, engines, fortifications, trenches, and in the demolition of them all, that this war mainly consists. Does the American soldier take kindly to the pick and shovel, the stone hammer and the drudgery? To ask that question is to answer it.. It is just because this war is so largely industrial that the German is so hard to beat. He is a past master at hard work. He is the genius of drudgery ALWAYS LOOKING FOR SHORT CUTS.

Along with this American lightness of step and mind, on the other hand, goes a quickness of intuition and imagination, which compensates to some degree at least, for lack of application to hard labor. If he does not succeed in gaining an end one way, he will try another. He does not believe in doing a thing just so because it always has been done that way. He is impatient of precedent, and inventive of short cuts.

Thus, for example, an officer newly come to Europe was discussing the strategy of this war with a veteran of one of the European armies, who told me of the conversation. Said the American:

"Do you mean to say that, when we have men enough, we can push the enemy back ten miles or so at a time, and then we must stop and bring up our railways and supplies, our guns and ammunition and get ready for another push?"

"That is it, exactly," replied the European.

"Then," said the American with finality, "we must find some other way." AMERICANS TO SOLVE PROBLEMS.

There is the case in a nutshell. This American did not know what the other way should be, but he fell to wondering, pondering. Out of that mood of inquiry finally would take shape some sort of tentative solution. And it was that same European who, by the way, is an engineer, who said to me:

"The war must finally be won by American ingenuity, invention, genius. The Americans must find some other way. Back in the laboratories and factories they must put their brains to work, comparing notes with one another and stimulating one another, to devise new expedients and solve this problem."

Many things of this nature have already been put into use, and many more will be forthcoming. The American will not be satisfied with tried expedients. He will seek the new. To be sure, he will use, and does use what has been found effective; he is no fool and is in Europe to learn. One thing that has astonished the older people over here is the open mindedness of the American officer and soldier. The Europeans thought the American would come over opinionated and cocksure, unwilling to listen to others or take suggestions; instead of which they found him silent, interrogative, thoughtful, knowing that he needed guidance, at least at first, and seeking it.

MAKE THEMSELVES AT HOME.

Yes, the American soldier is *sui generis*. There is a stamp upon him; and even without his uniform you would know him by the cut of his jib. Although his accent may be strangely German, Scandinavian, Italian, what not, there is an air and a manner about him that is distinctly American. I approached a sergeant the other day with an inquiry, and met a French accent. He spoke better French than English, this sergeant, and was a creole from Louisiana. He looked and acted, however, as American as any lad on the horizon.

Some of these boys, most of them, have never been out of their native states, but they make themselves entirely at home, and are getting an education. There are the East Tennesseeans, whose fathers were excellent riflemen in the Civil War. One of their officers told me these boys were taken from their home, knowing nothing of the war, its causes, its objects, not even knowing there was a war until they were called to the colors, ignorant of what it was all about, and plunged in a few weeks into the stream of world events, until their eyes were shocked open. A detachment of these mountaineers was put on a train near their homes. They were shunted around for three or four days, and dropped down near Greenville, N.C. The ladies of the town gave them a little garden party, and in talking with the men, said:

"Where are you boys from?"

"We're from America," answered the mountaineers. They thought they were in France and talking to French women.

ALL STRANGERS TO HIM.

This makes me think of the story "Marse" Henry Watterson told me in Louisville long after his quarrel with President Wilson over the Colonel Harvey incident. He was in Washington one day and the President sent for him for luncheon. Watterson was willing to bury the hatchet and went. In the talk that followed luncheon Colonel Watterson told the President how he was one day in the mountains of Kentucky or Tennessee and met a man who had never been outside the sound of his own dinner bell. He asked the man if he had ever heard of George Washington.

"No'p," was the reply.

"Know Abe Lincoln?"

"No'p. Nobody round here knows him, I reckon."

Ever hear of Mark Twain?"

"No'p. Don't reckon he ever lived in these parts, did he?"

"What!" cried the colonel. "Never heard of Tom Sawyer, Huckleberry Finn, Pudd'n Head Wilson —"

"Oh, yes," interrupted the mountaineer. "I voted for him."

The President laughed heartily at the joke.

When Dad was fighting in France, there was a German soldier who was shot through the windpipe. Dad crawled over to him and helped him all he could. He stayed with him until he died. All my dad said was, "He was fighting for his country as I was for mine."

MAN RUNS A FOOT RACE
Middle West Soldiers Fought Three Hours To Start the 'Show'
Wire Entanglements and Machine Gun Nests in Wood in St. Mihiel Salient Cost Lives of Seven Officers.

By Herbert Corey.

WITH THE AMERICAN FIRST ARMY IN THE ST. MIHIEL SALIENT, Sept. 19 (by mail). —There was a three hours' fury of fighting when the men of a certain Middle Western regiment attacked on the morning of September 12. Then there was a foot race for twelve kilometers. The regiment only took 180 prisoners. The boche had too good a start.

Like the other regiments of the division which formed the point of the advance in the St. Mihiel angle, this regiment attacked on a battalion front of half a mile. Regimental headquarters was so near the front line that a stone might have been thrown into it. Battalion headquarters was actually on the front line — on the toe of a little hill which thrust out from the Bois de Jurey toward the 300-yard wide valley through which the Westerners were ordered to advance to take the thin woods of the Bois de Sennard on the other side.

The wood itself was but four hundred yards deep. A strong belt of very heavy wire ran through the valley at a distance of 100 to 150 yards from the shallow first line trenches to which the Westerners were marched at 4 o'clock on the morning of September 12. In spite of the excellence of the American barrage this wire had not been cut. Shortly before 5 o'clock wire-cutting parties were sent out with their heavy nippers to start holes through it.

IOWANS IN LEAD.

M.A. Tinley of Council Bluffs was stationed at the top of the hill, overlooking the valley. He saw the men go over when the whistle sounded, with Guy S. Brewer of Des Moines in the lead. From the other side of the valley the machine guns quickened their fire. They had been playing upon the American lines, but when the barrage lifted, they knew the Westerners had started. They swept the line of wire.

Seven officers were killed before the men got to the wire. Brewer's runner dropped. Private Phelps of Red Oak, Ia., sprang to his side:

"I'll run," said Phelps.

The message carrying was not to a place of safety, but to the battalion P.C. on the toe of the hill. Other runners were killed or wounded, but Phelps kept on. More were needed, and Private Austin O. Russell of Red Oak volunteered. Here the Germans made perhaps the stiffest resistance along the entire St. Mihiel line, thanks to the uncut wire and an advance of position.

The time came when Brewer had to return to the battalion P.C. Before he did so, he called his senior captain and gave him his instructions. The line went on. It was at this time that a major was wounded and Capt. Percy M. Lainson of Council Bluffs took command of the battalion. Before he got through the wire to the wood, he met a line of machine gun nests.

FIRED FROM MEN'S BACKS
Ottawa, Kas., Soldier's Scheme Routs Boche, "O.P.H." Writes.
With 37-Pound Machine Guns Strapped Parallel to Four American Spines the "All Kansas" Pushed Through Five Miles.

(From The Star's Own Correspondent.)

WITH THE FIGHTING AMERICAN ARMIES, Sept. 21.— In making an advance, the infantry, while it has more obstacles to overcome, isn't encumbered like a machine gun outfit, and under ordinary circumstances the "doughboys" move faster than the machine gunners, who must carry their heavy guns and thousands of rounds of ammunition with them. But there was one machine gun company I know of that kept pace with the infantry all the time, and that was the one attachment to an "All Kansas" regiment, a company formed of Kansas boys, trained at Camp Funston.

In a report made to a high unit commander by another unit commander, the work of the company was highly praised, and especially the work of one platoon, commanded during the battle by Sergt. Clyde G. Latchem of Ottawa, Kas. The sergeant didn't start out in command of the platoon, but the lieutenant was forced to leave it in his charge while he took over the company. Sergeant Latchem had heard of the boche being chained to their machine guns, had heard of them putting machine guns in trees and attacking the enemy, had heard of the boche machine gunners carrying them on their backs and performing other feats with the little death dealers. He had an idea and determined to try it out with his platoon.

Machine gun carriers are ordinarily big, husky fellows, and the kind of men they raise in Kansas are particularly adapted for that kind of work. Pitching wheat and hay is great training for the development of the arms and shoulders of machine gun men. At the first opportunity, the sergeant called his four carriers together and explained his scheme, asking them if they cared to take a chance on it.

"Sure," they replied in unison. "It's great. We'll put it all over the rest of the fellows."

So the scheme was carried out.

Each of the carriers had a Vickers machine gun, weighing thirty-seven pounds, strapped on his back, and strapped permanently, so it couldn't fall off or shift its position. The barrel of the gun was placed parallel with the men's spinal columns, the end of the barrel even with their heads. The gunners, ammunition carriers and the other members of each section followed closely upon the carrier. When the time came to fight, the carrier dropped on his stomach, slipped his helmet on the back of his head so the flash from the gun wouldn't burn his neck, and lay quiet. The gunner dropped behind him with his shoulder to the butt of the gun; the ammunition men were on one side, where they could feed the gun as rapidly as necessary. Whenever the gunner wanted to shift his aim a trifle, he would call to the carrier:

"Head right," or "head left," or "head up."

In this way the platoon had no trouble in keeping up with the infantry, could get into action in nothing flat, and could vacate a position just as quickly as the doughboys. There was no digging in for shelter, no continual shifting, no ranging, and no necessity to pack and unpack, all of which takes time. And time is a valuable essential when you are chasing boche soldiers all over the country and when the "doughboys" ahead of you are depending upon the steady rain of your bullets to assist them in tight places.

"It worked like a charm," the sergeant told me after it was all over. "The boys never had so much fun in their lives, and they never got into action, or out of it, so quickly in their lives. We are always going to work it the same way in the future, because it delivers the goods."

The machine gun company, one platoon of which was assigned with each company of one of the battalions of the "All Kansas" Regiment, certainly gave a good account. Time after time most of the platoons had to stop and dig in. They did, even if it were necessary to use helmets, mess kits, knives, forks, spoons, fingers, anything.

One time one of the platoons bumped right up against a boche battery in action. It was a battery of .77s, those little fellows that correspond to our 3-inch guns.

It was a rather ticklish position, this business of attacking a battery of artillery with machine guns, especially when the artillery could blow you to smithereens in less than no time. But the men dug in and cut loose, and it wasn't very long until those boches who were left of the gun crews had to take to their heels. The machine gunners had captured an entire boche battery of artillery.

CUT OFF HUNS' RETREAT.

At another time the machine gunners got in advance of the infantry, while the infantry was trying to take a small town held by the boche. The platoon slipped around to the opposite side of the town and covered the only road leading back to bocheland with their guns, and then, when the Heinies decided to evacuate they found the back gate closed with a curtain of machine gun fire. Some of them tried to pass it, but failed. The rest stopped, and the infantry took two hundred prisoners out of the place.

The first six hours of the advance the machine gun company, all Kansas men, covered a distance of five miles, always going forward. These men have been mentioned so far in reports for the good work they did, and more will be mentioned later:

Sergeant Latchem, Sergt. Marshall Peterson, Kansas City, Kas.; Sergt. W.S. Griffith, Galva, Kas.; Private Frank Davidson, Merriam; Henry Daume, Haigler, Neb., and Herbert Foster, Liberal, Kas.   — O.P.H.

U.S. Marines, in France, burying enemy dead.

A MACHINE GUN OF THE 140TH WORKING IN THE DARK.

(From The Star's Own Correspondent.)

WITH THE MISSOURI AND KANSAS TROOPS, Sept. 25. — This photograph of a machine gun manned by Kansas City men of the old 3d Missouri was taken by flashlight while the gun was in action. In fact, there was a number of guns in action that early morning. The Huns started the party by throwing a few bursts of lead at us. Some French planes were overhead trying to cross the boche line, and shrapnel was dropping all around us.

The machine gun outposts are always slightly in the rear of the advanced infantry outposts, where they can cover the enemy lines and No Man's Land with a curtain of fire. When the infantry outposts retreat to the first line, the machine gunners usually must hold their points and pour steel into oncoming enemy in an endeavor to turn them back or reduce their number to such an extent that they can easily be handled by the infantry. The men in the photograph are using a French machine gun. — *O.P.H.*

A Mendon, Mo., Boy
Got His Hun

Private Tyson G. Nichols, son of Mr. and Mrs. J.W. Nichols, of Mindon, Mo., was the first member of his battalion to take a prisoner. He went to France in June with the 89th Division.

YANKS ARE TREATED FINE
French See That Americans Don't Get Homesick.
Morale of Troops Excellent, Lieut. C.R. Born, Just Back From Verdun, Says — Think Only of Complete Victory.

Almost anywhere in France looks like the good old U.S.A., it was declared last night by Lieut. Charles R. Born, who arrived from overseas for a 10-day stay with relatives before reporting at Camp Mead, Md., to aid in the construction of new signal corps units.

"American soldiers are everywhere, and they have made themselves strictly at home in their new environment," said Lieutenant Born. "They don't give a fellow a chance to get lonesome or homesick, and neither do the people of France."

Lieutenant Born was with the Americans in the "big push" which began west of the Meuse, near Verdun, September 26, and he declared the fighting of the Americans was spectacular and gallant in the extreme. A never-give-up spirit pervaded the troops, he said, and in every mind was the signal of victory. Defeat was not contemplated, he said.

The morale of the soldiers is extremely fine, Lieutenant Born said, and while victory would be welcomed, it is not desired until the Hun is thoroughly beaten or surrenders unconditionally.

Before going to France, Lieutenant Born was with the Bell Telephone Company. He received his training at Camp Lee, Va., and became a member of the 305th Signal Corps, later attached to the 80th Division of the 1st Army.

According to prisoners, the Germans expected an armistice to go into effect at 3:30 Monday afternoon. They were amazed when our artillery fire increased and the infantry attacked. Many who expected to be fraternizing with Americans are now prisoners.

TOOK PRISONERS FROM FOUR DIVISIONS.

One American division has taken prisoners from four boche divisions in the past two days, including one of the best enemy outfits on the whole front.

There seems to be no end to the machine gun defenses. As fast as a series of these are wiped out, others are encountered and the artillery's work starts all over again.

YANKS GET A "STOPOVER"
England Serves as a "Side Switch" for Doughboys.
Before Going to Battle Front Americans Are Distributed Among British Camps, Awaiting Transports to France.

LONDON, Oct. 4 (by mail). — To facilitate American troop transportation, England is serving as a huge side switch on one of the chief military routes to France — a siding on which large numbers of American units are stored until sea transports are available to take them across the channel.

For hundreds of thousands of Middle Western, Eastern and Pacific Coast doughboys it constitutes a delightful stopping off place on their trip from New York to the battle field of Europe.

Between fifty and sixty camps, filled with American soldiers waiting to go to France, are scattered over all England, from the channel to the Scottish border. There are also camps in Scotland and some in Ireland.

AMERICAN RAILROAD MEN AID.

A staff of America's ablest railroad men is co-operating with British Army officers, distributing the soldiers among these camps, then picking them up again and forwarding them to France. At its head is Col. M.C. Kennedy of Chambersburg, Pa., president of the Cumberland Valley Branch of the Pennsylvania lines. Another Pennsylvania lines man, Capt. W.S. Franklin of Philadelphia, is second in authority. Chief of the entire organization is Major General Biddle, commander of all American forces in the British Isles.

MOVE THE TROOPS QUICKLY.

Without noticeable congestion of railways, this staff is able to remove an entire convoy of Americans to camp within a few hours after their arrival at an English port. And the convoys are coming in constantly.

Many of the camps are in the most beautiful districts, near quaint old cathedral towns, with histories running back to the time of Alfred; in peaceful farming districts, with their neat brick farmhouse and hedge bordered fields, and even among the highlands of Scotland.

MEN ARE WELL QUARTERED

In some camps the men live in barracks; in others, under canvas. By winter, army authorities hope to have every American soldier comfortably housed in a hut. A liberal policy of leave enables the doughboys to see some of the country from which so many of their ancestors came.

The only more or less permanent cantonment populations in England are for the various American aviation units in training for duty in France.

DIDN'T KNOW YANKS WERE "IN."
But When Repatriated Villagers Saw Sugar They Knew It.

By the Associated Press.)

WITH THE ANGLO-AMERICAN FORCES ON THE VALENCIENNES FRONT, Oct. 12. —The villages in Vaux Andigny knew that the Americans were in the war but did not know they were fighting. All of them rushed to meet the troops when the Americans entered, the people thinking the men were British. The Americans were kissed again and again. The more emotional of the villagers also kissed the soldiers' rifles and bayonets which had delivered them from their oppressors. The villagers offered the soldiers tea, and when the latter produced the sugar for it, the people all cried:

"Why, you must be Americans!"

There was another outburst of enthusiasm.

YANKS IN A HEROIC BATTLE
Grand Pre Was Captured After Terrific Hardships.
Sinking in Mud Halfway to Knees, Americans Pushed into Argonne Stronghold.

(By the Associated Press.)

WITH THE AMERICAN FORCES NORTHWEST OF VERDUN, Oct. 17. — The capture of Grand Pre by General Pershing's forces was accomplished under terrific hardships and with a heroism not hinted at in the brief announcement of the taking of this stronghold of the Germans north of the Argonne Forest.

On the northern bank they found broad mud flats into which they sank halfway to their knees. The Germans by this time had discovered their approach and opened a bitter machine gun fire, but the Americans pushed steadily on. Beyond the mud banks, which were crossed slowly and with the greatest difficulty, the Americans found the Germans and closed with them in a desperate bayonet hand-to-hand fight. Rifles often were used as clubs, and each man struggled to down his individual opponent.

DROVE RUNS INTO WOODS.

At 11 o'clock the Americans had completely overcome the enemy, had driven him into the woods north of Grand Pre and were in possession of the important rail head.

The Americans took the town primarily by outwitting the enemy by attacking without artillery preparation, which the Germans had expected, by wading the River Aire at four points instead of building bridges, by struggling through almost impassable mud step by step until suddenly on top of the amazed Germans and by driving them into a retreat after hand-to-hand fighting.

SMASHED IN WITHOUT BARRAGE.

The Americans had moved to a point within a short distance of Grand Pre and the Germans had destroyed the bridges over the shallow Aire as they retreated. The enemy obviously expected an artillery fire to preface any further attack, for his surprise was unfeigned when the Americans smashed into his positions.

The American attack began at 6 o'clock in the morning. The men moved forward in the shelter of the forest, reaching the Aire at four points agreed upon where the stream could be forded.

Without attracting the attention of the Germans, the Americans then waded into the cold water, which reached their waists and even higher, and pushed across the stream.

In its successful advance north of the Argonne Forest yesterday the American 1st Army reached Champigneulle, one mile north of St. Juvin. A little further east toward the Meuse they gained possession of the Cote de Chatillon.

East of the Meuse, the Americans moved forward in the Bois de la Grande Montagne, the summit of which they now hold.

NOW THE WOODS ARE CLEARED.

WITH THE AMERICAN ARMIES IN FRANCE, Oct. 17. — Fighting in the mud and rain, the Americans are threatening to force the Germans out of the remainder of the Kriemhilde line. The Yanks, advancing northward from Grand Pre, have practically cleared the enemy from Loges Woods and are approaching Beffu (two miles north of Grand Pre). They have passed La Mussarde Farm.

According to prisoners, the Germans expected an armistice to go into effect at 3:30 Monday afternoon. They were amazed when our artillery fire increased and the infantry attacked. Many who expected to be fraternizing with Americans are now prisoners.

TOOK PRISONERS FROM FOUR DIVISIONS.

One American division has taken prisoners from four boche divisions in the past two days, including one of the best enemy outfits on the whole front.

There seems to be no end to the machine gun defenses. As fast as a series of these are wiped out, others are encountered and the artillery's work starts all over again.

THE 353RD INFANTRY TAKES PART
IN THE MEUSE ARGONNE OFFENSIVE
—
THE FIRST BATTALION MOPS UP BANTHEVILLE WOODS

There was no delusion about the situation at the front when the 353rd Infantry moved up on the night of October 19, 1918. Reconnaissance parties had noted the intensity of the struggle in the numbers of unburied dead scattered about over their future sector. Field Order Number 82, of the 32nd Division under date of October 16th, announced advance on the left and included the following instruction for their own forces:

> "No ground now held will be abandoned, but if necessary to obtain more favorable positions, local advance may be made. The Commander-in-Chief yesterday personally gave instructions to the Division commander that every foot of ground gained must be held at all costs. And he desired this impressed upon all ranks. Every man who had individually worked forward will form a rallying point for others coming up and the ground so gained by small groups will be held to the last. No falling back from the present outpost line will even be considered."

This order in full had come down to the companies of the 353rd Infantry with the endorsement of Division, Brigade and Regimental commanders. While the phrase, "all shot to pieces," had been ruled out, there was plenty of evidence that the 32nd Division had suffered many casualties. The sector ahead was a desperate proposition.

It had been reported that the enemy was retreating at other points on the line. Military critics had said that this sector formed a pivot and if it gave way, the whole German army to the north would be lost. German orders were, therefore, to hold here at all cost. To our front was one "Bois" after another and the terrain a succession of hills and draws. The enemy had concentrated large numbers of machine guns and artillery with intent to hold. The machine guns protected by sniper's posts built in trees. Our enemy was on the defensive in possession of every natural advantage and fighting what he must have known to be a death struggle.

The First Battalion took the lead under command of Captain Portman. Captain Crump, broken down completely, had been evacuated to a base hospital. The route to the new positions led through open fields, past Gesnes, into the heart of Bantheville Woods just west of the town of Bantheville. On the line one company relieved a battalion, one platoon a company. It seemed all out of proportion, but such was the measure of casualties in the retiring division. Shelling was very severe and the First Battalion suffered quite a few casualties before reaching the positions. "D" and "C" Companies were on the outguard, supported by Companies "A" and "B" respectively. Reconnaissance, however, had been thorough and, once in the area, relief was effected within two hours after it wad been commenced.

Shelling continued with increased severity. Captain Portman was severely wounded while standing at the telephone in his Battalion P.C. Command passed to Capt. Allen

Barnett of "A" Company. Captain Portman reported back on foot to the Regimental P.C., and was evacuated to a base hospital. His services in the World War were over. In addition to the losses from artillery fire, machine guns took their toll. Woe to any man who stepped out into the open to survey the line which wound its way through the dense under-growth, marking the advance limits of the position.

On October 21st, it fell to the lot of the First Battalion to relieve troops of the 178th Brigade to the right. Reports indicated that they were in position some two hundred yards ahead. Inasmuch as the Second Battalion was already in contact with the enemy in their own position, sone confusion as to situation and procedure resulted. One thing, however, was clear — the woods must be mopped up before relief could be effected.

At this point in the narrative, it seems best to submit statements from official; reports. From the report of Major-General Wright on the Meuse-Argonne operations from October 19 to November 11, 1981, covering the situation just after the 32nd American Division had been fully relieved on October 19:

"The 89th Division had been informed that the Bois de Bantheville had been cleared of the enemy and that all that was necessary in order to completely hold these woods was to mop them up. It was found that these woods were held in force and that the mission assigned was not one of mopping up but was virtually an advance against strong and stubborn resistance.

"The afternoon of October 20th orders were received from Fifth Army Corps (Field Order No. 48) for the attack of the line Hazois Woods, Hill 253. General instructions required that the attack be made by one brigade with the second brigade in reserve. In preparation for this Field Order No. 35 was issued directing the 177th Brigade to take over the entire front, placing the 178th Brigade, with the Divisional Machine Gun Battalion, in Divisional Reserve. This relief was finally accomplished after midnight, October 21-22. The enemy's scattered stragglers and occasional machine gunners in the Bantheville Woods, and his persistent gas shelling through the east central part of the woods impeded the operation of the relief. ...

"On 21 of October, instructions were received ... to adjust the boundary line with the 42nd American Division. This was accomplished thru Field Order No. 37 by the leading brigade of this division taking over, on the night of October 21-22 the front as far as Tulerie Farm from the 168th Infantry, 84th Brigade, 42nd Division."

On the same day, October 21, 1918, at 15 hours, Field Order 38 was published directing that the two battalions of the 178th Brigade then engaged in mopping up the northern part of Bantheville Woods to complete the operation. When this mission was satisfactorily completed they were to be withdrawn and form a part of the Divisional reserve. On the night of the 21st of October, the First Battalion of the 353rd Infantry completed the relief of the units of the 178th Brigade except two companies of the First Battalion of the 356th Infantry which remained in a forward position.

Terrific shelling and gassing together with close-up machine gun and sniper fire from all directions, indicated that the woods had not been cleared of the enemy. Relief could be effected only with great difficulty and severe losses. The situation was reported to Brigade Headquarters. An order came in reply directing First Battalion of the 353rd Infantry to advance to the north edge of Bantheville Woods and clean the woods of all the enemy. The time for the jump-off from the funk holes which had been occupied by the relieved elements was set for one o'clock without barrage.

Companies "A," "D," "C" and "B" formed in line from the western to the eastern edge of the woods along the general line ordinated from east to west as 87 on the Buzancy map. In the morning of October 22, the day of this advance, the two companies of the 356th Infantry moved northward in the woods and were located in the northern and eastern interior of same where they were practically cut off until the time of their relief by our advancing companies later in the day, as they passed through their positions to the edge of the woods.

Extracts from the original field messages were sent back by the Company Commander after receiving their objectives are indicative of the opposition they encountered before reaching their objective extending along the road bounding the northern edge of the woods.

YANKS KEEP BORING IN

Huns in Argonne-Meuse Sector Driven Slowly Back.

Americans, Fighting Against Great Odds, Are Crushing Kaiser's Best Troops, Frederick A. Smith Says — Doughboy Heroes.

BY FREDERICK A. SMITH

WITH THE FIRST AMERICAN ARMY, OCT. 30. — Standing today in a cold, clear sunshine, I looked out upon the hills and valleys where the Americans are fighting the greatest battle of our history, seeing pictures that made the breath come quick and made the heart swell with pride.

Into the strongest defensive positions on the West front the Germans have thrown nineteen divisions, sending general Von Marwitz down from Flanders to command them, with orders to stop our men on the Argonne-Meuse sector. Von Marwitz was selected because he was one of the kaiser's ablest generals.

There have been recurrent counter attacks upon us, but they have been smashed, although several have been engineered with strong forces. We have held the ground already wrested from the enemy and have persistently and heroically swept back upon the German lines, bidding, against the most desperate ventures of the enemy, for a further advance in the khaki line.

TAKE MACHINE GUNS.

There was a spectacular success at St. Mihiel when in six hours was claimed a great salient. It was a glorious feat to capture Mont Faucon and Forges Wood on the first day of this greatest American victory. There is still a "noble meaning" in the way the Americans are rushing against positions, some of which are seemingly as hopeless as Gallipoli.

Supported by pits, trees and trenches, the foe in Largave Wood have learned that American attacking can inflict equal losses on Germans defending. The bodies of Von Marwitz's soldiers dot with gray the slopes of Hill 299.

The eastern end of Bois de Foret is No Man's Land, a wilderness of German wire, impassable roads, and blanked by machine guns. On Hill 294 there is an enemy observation tower protected on the edge of the wood by machine gun nests, but our artillery has found its range, and today it stood upon three legs, the fourth having been cut away by a direct shell hit. The exploits of our men in Bois Belleau east of the Meuse already have been related.

This is a 30-mile battle line in which the struggling divisions are mostly hidden by the wooded country. It is a battlefield where the kaiser apparently is forced to the conclusion he must hold the Americans here or he cannot hold the Allied line anywhere. Whether he can stem the tide or not may be judged from the individual courage and spirit shown by our men.

WHY THEY WIN.

I recently saw a doughboy enter a dressing station, standing awkwardly by while the doctor attended a wounded man. The doctor thought the doughboy was a stretcher bearer and asked him what he wanted. The doughboy said he wanted a cigarette, but continued to stand around after he got it.

The busy doctor asked him to sit down, but the doughboy said:

"I can't, doc, I am a little hurt."

Examination showed part of both legs blown away, and when the doctors hastened to start to undress the doughboy and give first aid, he motioned them away, saying:

"Wait a minute, there's a guy outside who needs you."

He went out of the dugout and there, lying on the ground, was a comrade whom the doughboy had actually carried out of the battle lines on his back, despite his own desperate condition.

"THE TERRIBLE" DIVISION.

I have written much of how the 32d Division boys carried Juviegny with a dash fully justifying the name applied to them by General Mangin when he requested in August that they be rushed north of Soissons at the beginning of the drive whereby the French cleared the famous Chemin des Dames. He called these Michigan and Wisconsin boys "Les Terrible," and so they are.

The doughboy who carried his pal out of the front line on his back was one of these. Two other diminutive runners known as the "Terrible Twins," because both came from Marshfield, Wis., and they always worked together. While among the smallest of the soldiers in the army, they are big in courage, and while both have German names, they are steadfast in Americanism.

NOT SMALL ENOUGH.

They are Frank Die and Fred Freund, and when I asked them if, while carrying messages to and from the battle fields under constant machine gun and artillery fire, they did not sometimes thank the Almighty they were so small, Die said:

"No, we pray to him to please make us a little smaller."

These regiments went through the furnace of fire on Hill 230 in the second Marne battle before they were rushed up to help General Mangin in the Soissons country. Thinking of them as fierce visaged warriors would hardly be justified, because they are first with a smile.

Four of their stretcher bearers, who travel through fighting areas together, are college graduates. They carry their winning ways into No Man's Land. Two of these college men were carrying a stretcher, assisted by two captured Red Cross men, when a third Red Cross man addressed the Americans and said they should not be doing such work and, if they would wait a minute, he would get four German prisoners to take the wounded man to our dressing station.

ALL COME BACK.

It looked like a ruse by which the German hoped to escape, but he seemed sincere and he was told to go and try, whereupon he went into the wood and returned with four Germans who relieved the Red Cross men of the burden, and the little company of three Americans and seven Germans trudged back through the wire land together.

It would require many columns to give the details of how ennobling to the meaning of the word American are the deeds of this army. It is the work here that will cause the hats to come off over there when the signal corps men, engineers, runners, telephone squads, aviators, doughboys, supply train men and offices have these hills where the wind and rain are cold, but the fire of patriotism burns so cheerily.

TONS OF STEEL ON GERMANS.

The American Big Guns Had Their Best Day Yesterday.

(By the Associated Press)

WITH THE AMERICAN ARMY NORTHWEST OF VERDUN, Nov. 1 (delayed) – Hundreds of tons of steel were fired by the big American guns in the direction of the railroad centers at Conflans, Longuyon and Montmedy and other points today, in co-operating with the infantry attack west of the Meuse. The guns began firing early in the morning and kept up their bombardment all day. It was said to have been the busiest day that the guns have had as yet.

YANKS FIND MANY DEATH TRAPS.

Thermometers, Clocks and Canes were Connected with Explosives.

(By Edwin L. James)

WITH THE AMERICAN ARMY, Nov. 1 (delayed) – Boche humility continues to be illustrated by the high class infernal machines he leaves behind. The ingenuity of these seems to depend upon the time Heinie had to work it out. In some regions every dugout has its little contrivance of death; but of all the assortment , the one he left at Chatel-Chehery ranks first. It was here that ammunition dumps and dugouts began to explode two days after the Germans left the place some two weeks ago. Ten days after the enemy had left, two dougouts blew from time bombs. Our engineers have found many types of infernal machines, such as those fixed to 8-day clocks and the thermometers.

For ingenuity, one found yesterday was remarkable. Eight feet from the entrance of a handsome dugout that would make a good shelter for weary doughboys was found a cane, hanging carelessly over the balustrade of a stairway. It looked harmless, but a certain engineer lieutenant had learned to be wary. Walking around the cane, he examined it. It appeared to be all right. Turning on his flashlight, he went over it minutely, and halfway between the ferrule and the handle he saw a small black string tied. This string led to the balustrade and down to where a person would naturally stand at the foot of the stairs when grasping the cane. Beneath this spot, four feet square, a hole was filled with an explosive corresponding to TNT.

That is one illustration of how the boche likes to fight.

That is one of the reasons why the doughboys think less favorably of all armistice than they might otherwise.

FLEE BEFORE YANKS
At Some Points West of Meuse Retreat Is So Rapid Americans Nearly Lost Contact.
ENDED A BITTER BATTLE
All Morning Long the U.S. Troops Everywhere Had Met Stubborn Resistance. Despite That, However, a 4-Mile Advance Was Made in the Afternoon.

FOSSE FALLS TO AMERICANS
The Red Cross Is Delivering Emergency Rations to Advanced Positions by Air.
(By the Associated Press.)

WITH THE AMERICAN FORCES NORTHWEST OF VERDUN, Nov. 2. — The German forces are giving way before the pressure directed against them by the Americans. The Germans tonight are in retreat beyond the Freya positions.

The Germans have retired so rapidly at some points that the Americans have experienced difficulty in maintaining contact with the enemy.

THE AMERICANS TAKE FOSSE.

General Pershing's forces continued their attack upon the region west of the Meuse this afternoon and captured Fosse. This represents an advance of four miles from the starting line through Bayonville.

The Germans gave little if any indication of an impending retreat until this afternoon. All morning long the Americans on every part of the front had met with stubborn resistance.

GET RATIONS BY AIRPLANE

WASHINGTON, Nov. 2. — American aviators now are delivering Red Cross emergency rations to American soldiers in the front lines, who are pursuing the enemy at such a rapid pace that they have outdistanced army supply wagons. A dispatch today from France to the American Red Cross said by flying low the aviators are enabled to drop packages and newspapers at points where the soldiers are certain to get them.

THE 89TH IN ACTION AGAIN
Kansas and Missouri Boys Are Between Argonne and Meuse.
In making the announcement, General March said he had had no reports from the 35th Division since October 10.

WASHINGTON, NOV. 2.—The last word from the 89th Division (composed mainly of drafted men from Kansas and Missouri) disclosed it in the line between the Meuse River and the Argonne Forest, now prominent in the latest war dispatches. The 89th was reported in that position as recently as October 29, General March, chief of staff, said in his weekly conference with newspaper men today.

The 89th Division was last identified at St. Mihiel, where it participated in the drive in which that salient was pinched out. The 89th first went into the line in August, taking over a sector of the line in the Vosges Mountains, north of Toul, going from there to the St. Mihiel salient.

There was one time when Dad was visiting in town, the *Oberlin Herald* editor wanted to put all medals that servicemen received in the Herald window. There was a man who walked up to Dad and said, "George, didn't you get the Distinguished Service Cross?"

My dad informed him that he knew nothing about it. When he arrived home, he informed my brother and me that if someone asked you about medals, you know nothing. He never talked about war.

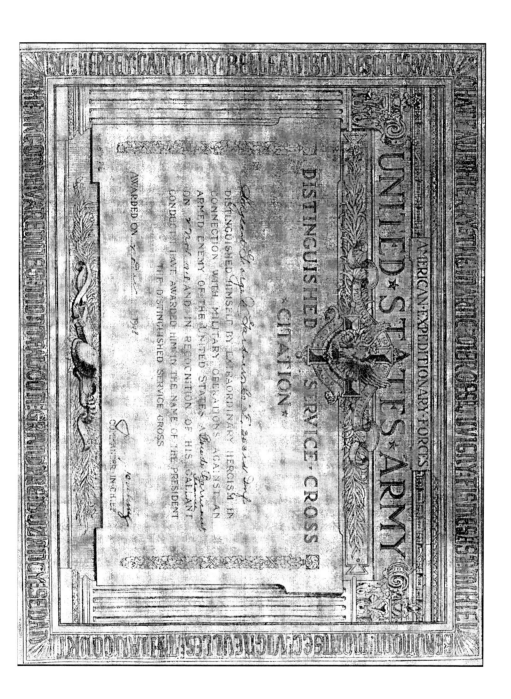

CROIX DE GUERRE

From Wikipedia, the free encyclopedia
(Redirected from Croix de Guerre)

The **Croix de guerre** is a military decoration of both Belgium and France which was first created in 1915. The decoration was awarded throughout World War I and again during World War II. The Croix de guerre was also commonly bestowed in foreign military forces allied to France and Belgium.

The Croix de guerre may either be bestowed as an individual medal or as a unit award. The Croix de guerre medal is awarded to those individuals who distinguish themselves by acts of heroism involving combat with enemy forces. The medal is also awarded to those who have been "mentioned in dispatches," meaning a heroic deed was performed meriting a citation from an individual's headquarters unit. The unit award of the Croix de guerre was issued to military commands who performed heroic deeds in combat and were subsequently recognized by headquarters.

Further acts of bravery resulted in the award of additional medal insignia worn on the ribbon of the medal; the ribbon being green ribbed with seven red stripes.

French Croix de Guerre of World War

Appearance

The Croix de guerre medal varies depending on which country is bestowing the award and for what conflict. Separate French medals exist for the First and Second World War, and the French medals are different in appearance from the Belgian design.

For the unit decoration of the Croix de guerre, a fourragére is awarded which is suspended from the shoulder of an individual's uniform.

Because the Croix de guerre is issued as several different medals, and as a unit decoration, situations typically arose where an individual was awarded the decoration several times, for different actions, and from different sources. Regulations also permitted the wearing of multiple Croix de guerre, meaning that such medals were differentiated in service records by specifying *French Croix de guerre, Belgian Croix de guerre, French Croix de guerre (WI),* etc.

Degrees

The Croix de guerre was awarded with various attachments, depending on the command level of the awarding authority.

For French *Croix:*

• a bronze star for those who had been cited at the regiment or brigade level.

When Dad was fighting in France, there were times when there was not enough food, so they would eat moldy bread, not realizing it was penicillin. When hungry, you would eat almost anything.

You would never know what would be in any fox hole. When jumping in one, my dad was shot between the shoulder blades, but would not go back to the Red Cross to be treated. He always said he would lose the 89th Division and the 353rd Infantry. The only time he did go back to the Red Cross was when he tried to see his brother, Jonas R. Gardner, but he missed him as he was already on his way on a ship heading for the U.S. His brother was shell-shocked for 33 years. Dad always said he wished his brother had been killed with all the turmoil that he went through.

The photograph shown above was widely printed in the German press at the time the Germans captured their first batch of American prisoners. Cyrus E. Dallin, the sculptor, was struck with the defiant way in which the central figure — a corporal, as shown by the chevrons on his sleeve — faced his captors, and forthwith set out to model the figure shown on the first page of this issue of the Post-Dispatch Sunday Magazine. The picture also is not devoid of other character studies, as note the gloomy expression of the young American soldier on the extreme right, and the triumphant grin on the face of the German officer at the left.

YANKS MEET STUBBORN OPPOSITION

WITH THE AMERICAN ARMY ON THE SEDAN FRONT, Nov. 4. — In the face of stubborn opposition the Americans took and held firmly the wooded heights south of Beaumont, the last German stronghold west of the Meuse. The advance carried the lines forward for an average gain of five kilometers (three miles).

The forces on the heights are now only about seven and one-half miles from Carignan, on the Mezieres-Metz Railroad, and about nine miles from Sedan, bringing both places within range of the Allied shell fire.

The day's work may be said to have been complete. It was the principal phase of the American operation since the neck of the German lateral communications between the armies to the north and west was narrowed to the strangling point.

CRASH THROUGH CENTER

The attacking forces to the right and left advanced with less speed than at the center, where an American division crashed through, despite the most stubborn opposition offered by the Germans since the beginning of the offensive. The apex of the line was driven to the heights, which are vital, affording dominating positions for the artillery.

Patrols went into and beyond the town itself, but its possession is unnecessary, as long as the hills are held by the Americans. The Germans cannot fight over the terrain north and northeast, because of the lack of communicating lines there. They must fall back as soon as the American artillery breaks up the remaining railroads, even if the main lines from Sedan to Metz are not smashed first.

END TO PRESENT OPERATIONS

The military authorities were overjoyed with the result of the day's fighting, declaring that it may even spell the end of the present operations, and that any others to the north, westward or directly eastward would constitute entirely new operations.

The American left wing pushed forward slowly, but doggedly. The Americans occupied Verrieres and Oches. The right wing worked its way down the River Meuse and reached a line between Beaufort and Beauclaire and north of Halles and Wiseppe. This flank met with the most stubborn resistance from the enemy, who fought bitterly to prevent encroachment on the important town of Stenay.

American troops in mass made no effort to cross the River Meuse. Patrols encountered heavy machine gun and artillery fire at every attempt. They remained at nightfall upon the west bank.

The center moved so fast that they took prisoner German re-enforcements coming to aid their comrades in the front lines.

YANK AIRMEN DOWN THIRTY.

Squadron of 145 Planes Attacked Montmedy — Seven Americans Missing.

(By the Associated Press)

WITH THE AMERICAN ARMY NORTHWEST OF VERDUN, Nov. 4 – In aerial fighting today between American and enemy machines thirty German airplanes were brought down and three balloons destroyed. Seven of the American planes are missing.

Montmedy was bombed by a squadron of forty-five planes, which were protected by 100 pursuit planes this afternoon. Excellent results were obtained on the heavy enemy traffic behind the lines.

THE 89TH IN BATTLE NOW
Since Friday Morning, the Funston Division Has Been Fighting.
A Captured German Order Shows That Huns Consider Westerners as Good Shock Troops, O.P.H. Says.

(Cable from The Star's Own Correspondent.)
WITH THE 1ST AMERICAN ARMY IN FRANCE, Nov. 6 (delayed). — The 89th Division of the American Army, which was trained at Camp Funston, Kas., made such an excellent record in the present offensive and at St. Mihiel when the salient was wiped out, that the enemy himself has taken official cognizance of it.

The 89th started the present drive Friday morning. It advanced twenty-two kilometers (about fourteen miles) over difficult terrain and against strongly defended positions. The following extract of the official German orders was taken from the body of a Hun officer:

"This division (the German 88th) is again opposing the American 89th as at St. Mihiel. This division is known as a 'good American shock division,' which undertakes many strong patrol missions."
A REAL COMPLIMENT FROM GERMANS.

No better compliment could be paid the 89th Division than this enemy order. The 89th swept everything before it now as it did before, proving that the training it received at Funston was excellent. It fought continuously against the powerfully organized Kriemhilde line defenses across the entire front. That country is broken with ravines and hills and offers ideal terrain for enemy rear guard machine gun action and also heavy artillery resistance.

Yesterday the 89th captured Cesse and Beaumont, both strongly defended places, and then mopped up Jaulny, in the bend of the Meuse between Cesse and Beaumont. The attack began Friday morning at 5 o'clock, after two hours' artillery preparation. The 89th advanced six kilometers the first day and five the second day, which was five kilometers ahead of the corps' objective for that time. The heaviest resistance was met in Loges Wood and Champigneville.

The weather was excellent until the afternoon of the second day, when a heavy rain began. It cleared Sunday morning and the weather was excellent for observation and artillery work, but there was more rain Monday and Tuesday, making progress difficult. But in spite of the adverse weather conditions, our troops remains in high spirits and continued gaining ground against steadily increasing enemy resistance until five miles from the Sedan-Metz Railroad, one of the enemy's main lines of communications with Germany.

THE YANKS ADVANCE AGAIN.
Pershing Pushed His Right Wing Ahead in the Woevre.
(By the Associated Press.)
WITH THE AMERICAN FORCES ON THE MEUSE FRONT, Nov. 8 (6 p.m.). — The right wing of General Pershing's forces advanced today, pushing into the western edge of Eourey Wood and in the Woevre Forest.

In the Ecurey Wood region the whole line advanced, cutting off the salient of the Bois de La Montagne, Haraumont and Brandeville.

In the Woevre Forest sector it was patrols who penetrated the edge of the forest, and they met with resistance. This section of the battle line contains virtually the last strong enemy defensive positions. His withdrawal far to the rear is practically certain.

On the balance of the front the day continued to produce little activity save that displayed by machine gun and artillery.

THE 89TH HIT 7 DIVISIONS
Streaming Up the Meuse, Division Swept Everything Aside.

Maj. Mark Hannah Crossed on Bridge Girders Ahead of Troops To Keep in Contact with the Enemy.

(By cable from The Star's own Correspondent.)

WITH THE 89TH DIVISION IN FRANCE, Nov. 8 (delayed). — Seven different enemy divisions opposed the 89th Division in vain efforts to stop the Camp Funston troops in the first five days of their last offensive, along the Meuse River.

Prisoners from that many divisions were captured in the advance and were identified.

TOOK 1,759 PRISONERS IN FIVE DAYS.

Prisoners numbering 1,759, including fifteen officers, were taken in those five days.

Booty included fifty-nine cannon, 335 machine guns, a wagon train, a truck train and a large amount of ammunition.

Complete details are now released by the censor, showing the progress of the 89th Division in its last drive and the towns and villages freed by this division.

CLEARED OUT MACHINE GUNS.

The 89th's last drive started in the territory between Gesnes and Cierges, first clearing out the Gesnes Woods, which was filled with machine guns for rear guard actions by the enemy.

Romagne was captured next and the Romagne Woods cleared out as the division advanced to the north.

A battalion of troops from St. Joseph, Mo., and that vicinity was given the task of clearing out the Bantheville Woods. The men did it, and did it in a hurry.

Remonville was taken next, followed in close succession by a number of towns and villages as the division swung off toward the Meuse River, continuing its advance in a general north direction.

CAPTURED MANY TOWNS

Towns captured included Barricourt, Tailly, Nourat, Lechampy, Basle, Champy, Beauclair, Halles, Beaufort, Laneuville, Cesse, Luzy and Letanne.

Original plans of the division were for a drive straight to the north from the starting point, Gesnes and Cierges. Such a movement would have brought them to the Meuse River at Letanne.

Their advance was so rapid, however, plans were changed and the division swung toward the east, coming in contact with the Meuse River at Laneuville. From that city to Letanne they cleared the west bank of the river up to Letanne.

The river was at flood stage, and all bridges were destroyed, so no effort was made to cross with the troops.

Patrols, however, spent much time on the east bank of the river investigating the enemy's strength and systems of defense.

Maj. Mark Hannah, a Kansas City man commanding a battalion of Western Missouri troops, made a bold patrol visit into Pouilly in the fourth day of the drive.

Pouilly is on the east bank of the Meuse and was not captured. Major Hannah's troops were on the west bank of the river, across from Pouilly. Bridges had been destroyed, but girders were left standing.

CRAWLED ACROSS ON GIRDERS.

Major Hannah, accompanied by his orderly, crawled across the girders, a distance of a hundred yards. He stationed the orderly at the east end of the bridge to cover a retreat and walked boldly into the town. Major Hannah stood on a busy street corner in Pouilly, smoking cigarettes, while French civilians and boche soldiers passed by in great numbers. By the audacity of his performance he was not suspected and made a safe return, bringing with him valuable information as to the enemy's strength and activities.

PRAISE FOR GOOD WORK.

In the clearing of the Bantheville Woods, done by the St. Joseph and Western Missouri battalion, as related previously there was work done which brought the commendation of the 1st Army Commander, as well as lesser commanding officers. The army commander sent this letter:

Army commander directs you to convey to the commanding general, officers and men of the 89th Division his appreciation of their persistent and successful efforts in clearing the Bantheville Woods of the enemy.

The following endorsement was added by the corps commander:

In transmitting the enclosed letter to you, your officers and enlisted men, the corps commander desires to add his commendation to that of the army commander and to congratulate you on the morale and spirit of your division as shown by its recent work.

Maj. Gen. William Wright, commanding the division, added his commendation to other letters of praise, and all were distributed to the men of the division.

Among the prisoners there was one woman dressed in soldier's uniform. No further details on this incident are available.

FOLLOWED CLOSE ON BARRAGE.

According to the story told by captured prisoners, the original barrage was extremely heavy and demoralizing. Our infantry followed so closely upon the heels of the barrage the boche had no time to reorganize to meet the infantry, after they had taken cover to avoid the artillery.

Further demoralization of the enemy resulted from their retreat being so rapid they went back into their own barrage, according to the tale related by captured prisoners.

At times their retreat was so rapid the infantry of the 89th could not overtake them, making it necessary continuously to send out patrols to keep in contact with the enemy.

Our artillery was the first to concentrate fire on the Sedan-Metz Railroad, one of the enemy's main lines of communication. This railroad runs parallel to the Meuse River, on the west bank.

THE 89TH NEAR SEDAN.
Funston Division Shared Glory with the Rainbow Men.
By Edwin L. James

WITH THE AMERICAN ARMY IN SEDAN,, NOV. 8. —Preparatory to our further advances the Germans are concentrating artillery fire on the heights north of the city. Farther east they are preparing strong positions on the heights north of the Meuse River. Thousands of the boche are at work building stone machine gun nests. In Martincourt several hundred of Germans were seen late today building defenses with material taken from the railroad embankments.

East of the Meuse we today captured Villesons, Hanaumont and Sivry and are pushing north. We have crossed the river at many points. There are no Germans on this side of the river in front of the 1st American Army.

The troops which reached Sedan are the 42d, Rainbow Division. Other divisions participating in our rush north are the 89th (Kansas, Missouri, Nebraska and other Western men); 90th (Texas-Oklahoma); 77th (New York); 78th (New Jersey-New York); 80th (Pennsylvania); 32d (Michigan-Wisconsin); 1st, 2d, 3d and 5th regulars; 26th (New England), and the 29th (New Jersey).

CAPTURED 89TH COLONEL
Levi G. Brown Taken Prisoner by the Boche.

(By cable from The Star's Own Correspondent.)
WITH THE FIRST AMERICAN ARMY, Nov. 11. — Lieut. Col. Levi G. Brown, operations officer of the 89th Division, was taken prisoner by the boches October 13.

General Brown is the only American general staff officers who has been taken prisoner.

His capture was effected by the Germans in the Bantheville Woods, near the town of Bantheville.

Colonel Brown was mapping the terrain ahead of the Camp Funston's division's advance toward Sedan when he was captured. He had been appointed only recently to the position of operations officer.

Accompanied by Private Charles Garrison, Garrison, Mo., Colonel Brown entered the Bantheville Woods just after the enemy had been cleared from that position. They were on horseback.

A detachment of the enemy made a counter attack, surrounding Colonel Brown and Private Garrison in the woods. Colonel Brown ordered Garrison to attempt his escape, which he did in spite of heavy machine gun fire.

Bosche prisoners captured the next day told of Colonel Brown's capture and said he was not injured.

Colonel Brown is a regular army officer, serving in the 13th Cavalry at Fort Riley before the outbreak of war, when he was assigned to the 89th division. He was an instructor in the first officers' training school at Fort Riley.   — *O.P.H.*

HAD ONLY 12 MEN LEFT
Capt. Mabrey Mellier Lost Nearly His Entire Company.
Kansas City Officer, Back To Recuperate, Tells of Gallantry of 89th Division at St. Mihiel and in Argonne.

To have in action only twelve men of his original company of 172 who left Camp Funston with him for France was an experience of Capt. Mabry Mellier, commander of Company C, 341st Machine Gun Battalion, 89th Division, who led his men until October 27 when he dropped on the field from exhaustion.

Captain Mellier, a Kansas Citian, now is recuperating in the post hospital at Fort Riley, awaiting discharge from the service.

NO BRAVER MEN IN WAR.

"The highest compliment I can pay the men of the 89th Division is that there were no better or braver soldiers in any army participating in the war," Captain Mellier said.

In the engagements of the Argonne and St. Mihiel, replacements for Captain Mellier's command were necessary three times. The casualties which reduced the original company to a mere handful were listed as killed, wounded and gassed.

The high regard of the enemy for Americans is shown by an incident told by the Kansas Citian. A captured German officer was asked if the Germans still believed God on their side.

"Yes, God is still with us, but the Americans are with the French," the German officer answered.

MEN LIVED IN "FUNK" HOLES.

From early in September to the last of October, Captain Mellier said, he and his men lived in "funk" holes, places they had dug to protect themselves from the fire of the enemy.

Captain Mellier entered the service in May, 1917, and was commissioned from the first officers' training camp at Fort Riley. He formerly was sales manager for the Faultless Starch Company.

When Captain Mellier was carried from the field, he was taken to Base Hospital No. 28, the Kansas City unit commanded by Lieut. Col. J.F. Binnie.

THE FRENCH LIKE AMERICANS

The French people like us militarily. They also like us politically. They like our democratic ideals, democratic ways, which is but another way of saying they like themselves, for in these respects the two nations are closely alike. France not only is a republic, but in some respects her democracy goes further than ours. Politically the two nations are closely akin. What the French people think of their president, Poincare, I do not know, but I do know what they think of President Wilson — they think he was the greatest living man in the world. Paris is not the only French city that has named a street in his honor. A similar recognition may be found within a block from the hotel where I am writing these lines. People tell me that never at the movies is Mr. Wilson's picture thrown upon the screen but that it is received with tremendous cheers. I am told further that President Wilson is as popular in Paris as Washington.

"RAG TIME" POPULAR

The American "rag" seems as popular in Paris as in New York. The American invasion is directed against the German, but the musical world of France has felt it first. It is truth to say that the "slap-bang" of the "Over There" is more in evidence in the capital of France than in our own capital.

Last night, going out in a train, one of our number, Dr. Harry C. Rogers of the Linwood Boulevard Presbyterian Church of Kansas City, an expert linguist, cried out to an old snow whiskered man as we passed out, *"Vive la France!"* and with a swift coming to attention, the old man answered, *"Vive l'Amerique!"*

A Kansas City man whose heart is still in Kansas City wrote home to his wife and went to a flower stall to purchase a rose to enclose in the letter. His French being uncertain, he carried the envelope and in the sign language made known his desire. The coveted flower was soon in his hand, but when he came to pay he was met with an astonishing "Nothing. I give it to you for the honor of France."

When the other day I came into one of the cemeteries where our American heroes sleep softly, tears were in my heart.

It was not the long level rows of mounds or the white marking posts that pulled mostly at my heart. It was the new plucked flowers on the grass, placed there by these French women.

ADOPT SOLDIER GRAVES.

For the moment they are ours," these gentle women say, "and what their own mothers would do for their graves if they were here, we shall do in their absence." I was strangely moved when I saw the names of our boys, and just beneath the penciled names of the women who call themselves "adoptees." They will care for, in beautiful mother way, the graves of those at whose heads they have written their own names. A simple white cross marks the grave, and on the traverse bar the name, date of birth and death and military identification of the soldier.

A GERMAN LETTER FROM THE FRONT

One of our readers, Mr. J.C. Krajicek, of Dodge, Nebr., sends in the following letter which is supposed to have been written somewhere on the western front by Crown Prince Frederick William to the kaiser, his father, back home. It is not guaranteed to be genuine, but it hits the situation off pretty well. Here it is:

Dear papa,

I am writing on the run, as the brave and glorious soldiers under my command have not seen the Rhine for so long that they have started back that way, and of course I am going mit dem.

Oh, papa, dere has been some offel dings happened in France. First, I started in my big offensive which was to crush de fool Americans, but dey know so little about military tactics dat dey will not be crushed like I want 'em. I sent my men in der fight in big waves, and when dey got to de Americans dey all said "Boo" as loud as dey could holler. Vel, according to vat you have always told me, de Americans should haf turned and run like blazes.

But vat do you tink? Dem fool American don't know anyting about war, and instead of running de odder vay, dey came right toward us. Some of dem vas singing about "Ve von't come back till it's over over dere," or some odder foolish songs and some of them laffin' like fools.

Dey are very ignorant. But dey are offel reckless mit dere guns, and ven dey come toward us it vas den dat my men took a notion dey vanted to go back to de dear old Rhine. Ve don't like de little old dirty Marne river anyhow.

And, oh, papa, dem Americans use such offel language. Dey know notting of kultur, and say such offel dings right before us. And dey talk blasphemy, too. Vat you tink dey said right in front of my face? One big husky from de place dey call Nebraska, he said — oh, paper, I hate to tell you vat an offel ting he said; but I can't help it. He said, "To hell mit der kaiser!"

Did you efer hear anyting as offel? I didn't tink anybody would say such a offel ting. It made me so mad, I vouldn't stand and hear such a offel ting, so I run mit the older boys. Vas I right? Vat?

And, oh, papa, you know dem breastplates vat you sent us — can you send some to put on our backs? You know ve are going de odder vay now, and breastplates are no good, for de cowardly Americans are shooting us right in de back. Some of our boys took off dere breastplates and put 'em behind, but de fool Americans are playing "De Star-Spangled Banner" mit machine-guns on dem plates.

Can't you help us? You remember in your speech you said notting could stand before de brave German soldiers? Oh, paper, I don't believe dese ignorant Americans ever read your speeches, for dey run after us just like ve vas a lot of rabbits. Vot you tink of dot?

Can't you send dem some of your speeches right away? Dey don't know how terrible ve are. Can't you move my army back to Belgium vere ve von all our glory? My men can vip all de vimmen and children vot dem Belgians can bring up. But dese Americans are so rough and ignorant. Ve can't make 'em understand dot ve are de greatest soldiers on earth, and ven ve try to sing "Deutschland uber Alles," dey laugh like a lot of monkeys.

But ve are getting the best of the Americans. Ve can out-run dem. Papa, if ve are not de best fighters on earth, ve are sure de best runners. Nobody can ketch up mit us ven ve tink of dear old Rhine, and my army never did tink so much of dot dear old river. Let us know right avay vat to do by return postoffice.

— Crown Prince Willie

PAPA ANSWERS CROWN PRINCE

Dear son Villie:

I got your letter a leetle vile ago bei der bost ofice, und listen to vat papa says.

Yes, it is an offel ting dat de American soldiers know noddings about war. Dat man, General Pershing, shows de American boys all de offel tricks you tell about such as to take aim, shoot mit der rifles und never go packwards. Did you ever hear of such a foolish ting? If de Chermans did not know how to go packwards, Villie, ver would dey pe now? Dey would all pe det, dat's vat.

Dis makes me tink apout dem breastblates which you dells we are in der wrong blace ven your run packwards. It will neffer do for de prave defenders of de Vaterland to half der pack exposed to der plasphemous pullets of der American swine. Listen to papa, Villie, und I vill tell you how to fix it. Take a trench schuffel und chust let it hang down on your pack und cover up what you don't vant to be shooted. Dis shuffel vill stop de pullets und you can laugh at de enemy und keep on running.

You say de American solchers use such offel lankwitch. Dey haf no kultur. Don't haf anyting to do mit dem, Villie. Chust run as fast as effer you can and keep avay from dem. If you get a chance to haf your men drop bombs on de Red Cross hospitals, dat's fine; dat's kultur; dat's pizness. I haf a whole sauer krout parrel full of iron crosses for my brave airmen who can hit a Ret Cross hospiddel right in der mittel.

Ve vant peace, hey, Villie? Papa means a Cherman peace, of course. Already I haf a cuppel of letters from de American bresident. He says in vun letter some dings aprout how peace can be hat if I gif de Cherman beeple more to say in de cufferment. Dat's easy for I haf already told de chancellor to let de beeple say all dey vant to, chust so dey haf no votes. Not so bad for paper. Hey, Villie?

De bresident wrote we an offel nice letter de first time but de next vun vas a leetle imbolite. Maybe he asked some odder beeples apout it und dey — vay you call it? — putted in dats it.

I heard dat de Republican party in America vants de Chermans to surrender uncondishionally und dey iss an offel mean party, don't you tink, Villie? Dey are meaner dan de Temmycrat party. De bresident iss going to try to keep de nasty Republicans out of his vay after dis. Dat vill be much nicer I tink. Den maybe I get some more letter bei der bost office.

Now, Villie, my prave poy, remember papa vants you to tooken gut care of yourself. Don't go near dem pullets but if you can't run fast enough be shure you vear de shuffel like I told you. So far paper's six poys are all safe.

Enclosed you will find annuder tecoration for your valor.

Your papa,
Kaiser Wilhelm Hohenzollern

HOME BOYS ON MEUSE
Peace Found Missouri and Kansas Troops Well Advanced.
Drive Toward German Border Was Progressing Rapidly,
O.P.H. Cables The Star of Final Activity of War on Hun.

(By cable from The Star's Own Correspondent.)
WITH THE AMERICAN ARMIES, Nov. 11 (delayed). — Progress of units of the 89th Division in the last three days of the last drive was substantial. They gained complete control of the Meuse River along their entire front, crossed the river and captured Stenay, Pouilly, Martincourt and other towns.

The division expects now to advance to the German border.

The present line was well in hand before fighting stopped.

CROSS UNDER FIRE.

A crossing of the Meuser River was effected under great difficulties.

Two battalions of the 355th Infantry crossed at La Neuville, paddling open pontoons.

Two battalions of the 356th crossed at Pouilly, going over single file across a shell-torn bridge.

The 353d Infantry crossed just below Stenay, going over on a pontoon bridge.

The 354th was covering the crossing of the other units, meeting the fire of the boche from the west bank. Crossing was made in the face of machine gun fire, hampered to some extent by the counter fire of the 354th.

In the taking of Pouilly, some men swam the Meuse, while others waded. Boche had blown out pontoon bridges as well as foot bridges.   — *O.P.H.*

CIVILIANS IN CHATEAU.

WITH THE AMERICAN ARMIES, Nov. 11 (delayed). — Upon entering Stenay today we found and visited the chateau occupied by the crown prince up to two months ago. The chateau was filled with hiding civilians.

Elaborate equippage is everywhere in this former home of the crown prince.

I have talked with a French woman who attended him. She says the crown prince was very pleasant and of good temper. Kaiser William visited the crown prince frequently, she says, and their visits were attended always by quarrels.   — *O.P.H.*

35TH IN REST CAMP

WITH THE AMERICAN ARMIES, Nov. 11 (delayed). — The 35th Division is in a rest camp and has been there since its fight in the Argonne Forest.

The celebrated Rainbow Division, including the Kansas City signal corps battalion and the Kansas ammunition train, is now hiking to a rest camp.   —*O.P.H.*

A RED CROSS STATION THAT SERVES THE 35TH.

With the Missouri and Kansas Troops — Never in the history of their lives will the young men who toiled up the steep mountainside that led to the trenches they were to occupy, forget the kindness and courtesy of the Red Cross. It was just about halfway up the mountain, on a wide spot in the road, the Red Cross decided to put its halfway station. It was only one tent, and a fly, the tent to house the men and their supplies, and the fly to act as a covering for the kitchen and counter, but it was enough. Regardless of the hour, there was plenty of good, luscious hot chocolate on the fire, and plenty of doughnuts. In addition there were magazines and newspapers, cigarettes and tobacco for the boys to take with them to the trenches. At night, when you saw a small illuminated red cross ahead of you, it always put more heart into your bosom and made your pack feel lighter. No one who ever climbed or went down the mountain has failed to stop there, whether generals or privates of the buck variety. The halfway station was a meeting place for all. — O.P.H.

RECOVERING FROM BOCHE GAS
American Barrage Terrific, Writes a Kansas City Sergeant.

Sergt. Chester Youngberg, Company L., 140th Infantry, 309 South Kensington Avenue, formerly employed in the bookkeeping department of The Star, writes:

I am in the hospital recovering from the effects of boche gas. I am able already to get out and walk around. We have been on the move since the first part of September. We were held in reserved at the St. Mihiel drive, but were not needed. September 23 found us behind the Verdun front. The night of the 25th we were ordered into action. There was an American bombardment going on and it kept growing fiercer.

The bombardment reached its climax about 5 o'clock in the afternoon and it gave us all the confidence in the world. By noon we were getting used to shells exploding about us and the music of the machine gun bullets cracking over our heads. We met stubborn resistance where a few machine gun nests had not been blown up. I lasted until the afternoon of the 29th. I was organizing a line and didn't pay any attention to a shell that exploded nearby. Several of us were put out by gas from the shell. I was blind two days, my lungs pained and I suffered from "seasickness." That has all gone and I feel fit again.

AVENGED A GAS ATTAC

Members of 89th Division Fought To Punisl

Members of the 354th and 355th Infantries Suffered Ma
O.P.H. Says — They Later Routed the Enemy at St

(By The Star's Own Correspondent.)

NANCY, FRANCE, Nov. 29. — With the Eighty-Ninth Division — Two days after the 89th took over the sector from Limey to Rangeval, the boche attacked with mustard gas, causing seven hundred casualties. The attack continued eight hours, and both the 354th and 355th Infantries bore the brunt of the attack admirably well. Two other regiments were kept in reserve. The boche began the attack early in the morning, using mustard gas mixed with high explosives. The shelling continued three hours, saturating the territory with gas.

The men wore masks and had moved to high ground when the shelling ceased. Two hours later the attack begin anew and continued three hour; again was saturated w so hours afterward.

The boches made hospital men and othe masks on to rescue tho

It was the divisior ence and also its firs fire. When taking the August 6, the boche f

Only a small percentage of the patients died. The men did not relish the gas and were wild to get after the boche when they later participated in the Saint Michiel-Verdun drives. They fought viciously and established a great reputation for the division.

THE 89TH LOSSES, 8,473

Kansans and Missourians Were in Line from August 6 to November 11.

(By The Star's Own Correspondent.)

WITH THE 89TH DIVISION IN GERMANY. Modifications in the military censorship now permit free mention of casualties for the first time since America entered the war. From August 6 to November 22 the 89th was in line the entire time, except two days. The entire casualties, including killed, wounded and missing, were 8,473, according to a report issued January 22.

The division entered the St. Mihiel salient August 6, and remained there during the entire drive, when the salient was wiped out. The casualties among the officers were: Killed, 16; wounded, 69; men killed, 281; wounded, 2,040; missing, 29. After the salient was consolidated, the division moved into the Argonne-Meuse attack, crossing the Meuse River the night before the armistice was signed. The casualties in this drive were: Officers killed, 29; wounded, 103; men killed, 771; wounded, 2,944; missing, 189.

— O.P.H.

NERVE AMAZED THE BOCHE.
Ambulance Men "Got the Jump" and Rescued Wounded Men.

WITH THE 89TH DIVISION, Dec. 1. — The road may be under fire, the area may be filled with gas, the ambulance drivers may have had only a snatch of sleep in days, but —

Here are a few scraps from a notebook that tells of the work of the ambulance companies with the 89th Division:

A boy had been lying out in No Man's Land two days with a broken leg, a little water in his canteen and a few hard biscuits. He had managed to bind up his leg with his first aid packet, but he had been unable to crawl to the lines.

Several times the boys had attempted to reach him, but a boche machine gunner had the place covered and each time drove them back. Victor Allen of Kansas City, driver of an ambulance, and Charles Grout, his orderly, volunteered. Allen drove his ambulance out into No Man's Land, stopped, descended and helped Grout bind up the man's leg so he could ride in the ambulance. The two placed the wounded soldier inside, then calmly turned around and drove back to the lines.

The boche were so amazed they didn't shoot for about two minutes, but when they did open up they sprayed the entire place. Several bullets struck the ambulance, but no one was scratched.

—

In the early part of the St. Mihiel drive four of the boys with the Kansas City outfit did such fine work in carrying in the wounded that they were mentioned especially in orders. They were stretcher bearers. Among those mentioned were Dwight Swanson, Oliver W. Holmes, G.D. Ferris and Lloyd E. Manning, all of Kansas City.

As early as St. Mihiel the Germans reported it as a new, but good, division.

When you come to figure it out, several things in this war are training back to a lonely old soldier in Kansas who was not allowed to come over. We do not know what they pretend to have on Leonard Wood, though a couple of people have tried to tell us, but this fact remains:

There are many thousand efficient officers in our victorious army who are, figuratively speaking, children of his brain, without whom we might not now have an army of occupation on the Rhine.

There is, moreover, in that army of occupation every division of fighting men he has trained. It seems to us that one man could not do very much more.

Sgt Geo H. Gardner
Co. F. 353 Ind.
A. P. O. 761.

(Nom et adresse de l'expéditeur.)

Sgt Geo H Gardner
Co F 353 Inf
Amer E. F.
A. P. O. 761

Soldiers
Mail.

CARTE-LETTRE

Miss Margaret Slocum
Dodge City
Kansas.
U. S. A.

Censored By

Sept 9 1918
France,
In a dugout
on the front
line.

Dear Friend.
It has only been a short
time since I wrote you but as I
have a few minutes spare
time and don't know just
when I will get to write
again will write a few
lines tonight. How I would
like to take a pleasure trip
like you have had. I'll bet
you enjoyed your trip. Well
I'll tell you I have one coming
as soon as the war is over.
Its strange that so many
of you old friends met
at Denver, and that lunch
you had. I sure would have
liked to been with you.
It would seem like

olden times. Well heres hoping
that I dont have to spend the
rest of my days in the army
and dont believe that I will,
but we never can tell we
can only see the past, dont
know what the future has
in store for us, am willing
to take my chances with
the rest of the boys wheather

they be small or great.
Suppose you are busy in
school these days well I
guess we all have to work
but dont work any more
than what is necessary
Thats the way I do

and I have always got
by pretty well.
Well I must close I have
to write to mother and nora
yet tonight and it is 10 oclock
But Fritz may send over
some of his canned 76
and disturb me before I
finish writing. You need
not wait for me to write
because my letters might be far
apart so write just when
ever you care to. Your letters
are always appreciated
Good Luck
as ever your
friend
P.S. Have been
in the army a few
days over one year
Sgt. G. W. Gardner
Co. I 353 Inf.
amer. Ex. F.
A.P.O. 761

CARTE POSTALE

La Correspondance au recto n'est pas acceptée par tous les pays étrangers
(Se renseigner à la Poste)

CORRESPONDANCE

ADRESSE

Fabrication Française GLORIA

M _____

Dear Friend
Am down in southern France oo
a ferlow just landed last nite so havent
saw much yet will write later and
tell you all about my trip. I am
Sgt G. W. Gardner Co. 7. 353 Inf, Yours Truly

WHEN THE 89TH WENT IN.
St. Mihiel Drive Started in Darkness, Soldier from M.U. Writes.
Americans Found Hun Army Living in Concrete Dugouts Equipped with Electric Lights — Beat Germans in the Air.

Lieut. Edward Klein of St. Louis, a former M.U. football captain, now with the field artillery in France, writes of the St. Mihiel drive, in which the 89th Division took part.

At 1 o'clock in the morning the heavies behind us and on both sides opened up. In spite of the continual booming of the guns, the screaming of the shells traveling through the air could be plainly heard. At 5 o'clock, the "H" hour for us, we opened up with a rolling barrage which we put down in front of our own front line trenches, and then continued lengthening it, and the infantry and marines went over behind it. We fired more than three thousand rounds in a little over three hours, and it really was a wonderful sight — quite dark when we started, and just the flashes of our own guns, the heavies in the rear, and other batteries like our own (field guns) throughout the field on either side of us.

ONE IN THE AIR.

Finally day began to break and the planes came up. Americans were knocking down Huns right and left. We surely had the supremacy of the air.

Our infantry went over so well that at 10 o'clock in the morning we hooked in and followed them — right across the field and over the trenches the Huns had occupied five hours before.

You never saw so much traffic, or such a sight in your life — four or five lines of guns, ammunition and food carts going forward, with reserve infantry cutting across the fields, and boche prisoners coming back on either side of the outgoing columns. Some were wounded, but for the most part they looked fairly happy, and seemingly glad that the war was over for them.

Then also there were streams of wounded Americans coming in, most of them able to come alone, and all happy and smiling. I wouldn't be anything but an American for anything in the world. Those who were too badly hurt to walk had four boche prisoners carrying each one on a stretcher.

FORCED BOCHE TO CARRY WOUNDED

I saw one marine being brought in that way, and he was quite pale, but was smoking a big cigar which he said he had "borrowed" from one of the prisoners who was carrying him.

We advanced and took a new battery position in a wood and fired again., all day and night, and then moved again, the third time.

Yesterday we were relieved, and while I am glad to be back in comparative rest, it was a good show while it lasted. I had my clothes off last night for the first time in ten days.

Our stable sergeant now has a German wagon and a nice boche team. He told me he was going to get a German coachman.

This salient had not been touched for four years, and the Germans had concrete dugouts, with electric lights.

—

AMMUNITION TRAINS CAN'T HALT.
When Battle Is On, They Must Deliver Shells, a Soldier Says.

Sergt. W.H. Knapp, 1532 Benton Boulevard, now with an ammunition train in France, writes:

From the Lorraine sector, which was comparatively quiet, we have moved to the Champagne. The men were comfortably settled in an old barn, half of which had been shot off, when shells came our way. Some were gas shells and we had to wear masks. Funny, but the thing I remember most was the awful thirst I had.

We were soon ordered to a nearby dugout to await our turn at carrying supplies to the men upfront. Just as we got in the dugout a large shell went off down the road a piece and left a hole big enough to drop four "Katy" freight cars in.

The shelling kept up till 8 o'clock the next morning, when the captain ordered us to take eighteen trucks back to a dump for ammunition. Well, it's a great life hauling high explosives during a big battle. Of course, if a shell hit you it would tear you up no matter where you were, but when you are on a truck you feel as if you were in more danger than anywhere else. On this occasion we were on and off duty for forty-one hours. None of our bunch was injured, but we saw a French truck blown into a million pieces. We also saw several dumps behind the enemy lines go up at night, which is great scenery.

One thing about ammunition trains that is different from other units is that when on duty we can't "duck" into dugout or get behind a tree when things get hot, but we have to stick right to the road and deliver our load, no matter what we see coming.

TELLS OF OPEN WARFARE
Kansas City Artillery Regiment Moves at Night, a Captain Says.

Capt. N.T. Paterson, with a unit in France under command of Col. Karl Klemm, in a letter to his sister, Mrs. F.W. Titterington, Twenty-ninth Street and the Paseo, tells of life in Forest d'Appremont, near St. Mihiel:

We are in the field, open warfare conditions, and without our dugouts that were so comfortable before. We have what we can carry and that is all, and at night no lights are allowed.

We are camped in the center of one of France's famous forests. Every precaution possible is taken against observation by enemy aircraft. The guns and pup tents are all camouflaged by trees, and whenever an airplane is sighted we all take to the trees. It really is an ideal camp, and we are getting good supplies of food. In the distance you can hear the roar of the guns, and at night the sky is lit up by the flashes and flares, together with numerous searchlights to detect airplanes.

We move at night and seek cover during the day. It is very exciting and enjoyable. There is a big railroad gun near us, and it keeps up its song all the time. The villages and cities near us are bombed constantly.

TOLD OF HIS FIRST DRIVE
Lieut. John Madden Heard the Boche Cry "Kamerad."

Artillery Preparation Competed with a Rain and Thunder Storm. Then Came Daylight and a Victorious "Over the Top" Charge.

Lieut. John Madden, 355th Infantry, 89th Division, formerly was a reporter for The Star and later editor of the Republic at Mound City, Kas. He received his commission at the first officers' training camp at Fort Riley. He writes:

Things happen quickly in the army. Here I am far back of the line sleeping on a real cot and eating at a real table — all out of artillery range — when three days ago I was writing in a dugout to the tune of shelling and gas alarms and machine gun bullets.

Probably we "crab" mores about the ages since the last bath, the fact that the nearest "Y" is finer, or bar chocolate or canned corn beef is too monotonous, than about the danger. The "why worry" theory about danger fortunately has been adopted universally by the American Army.

One imagines one knows a little of war when one exists in the front line or lives through a bombardment or gas attack or helps beat off an enemy raiding party, winging a few and picking up souvenirs such as pistols, grenades and guns, or is assigned to command a front line outpost past the forward trench in a No Man's Land town which is shelled every morning at 5 o'clock. These have been some of my experiences, but they melt into insignificance beside the ultimate event — the first participation in a formal prepared by artillery, guided by airplane advance, "over the top."

The night it happened I had two platoons in the town of ruins I spoke of when orders came that we would be relieved in that position and march to another advanced zone sector. The reason for the change was that our division which had been occupying a wide, quiet sector, was assigned a narrow slice of the wedge on the big night. Another division came in where I happened to be and all our troops were to be concentrated in one locality. Of course, the relief was last and didn't arrive until midnight. So there I was, with more than a hundred men, five miles from our destination an hour before the barrage started and expected to be in position for the jump-off by 1 o'clock. Not one of us had ever been over the roads or had seen the trenches we were to occupy.

It was raining. Oceans of water, subdued curses of mule drivers, frantic "Where is the —th infantry?" by lost details, troops marching everywhere, muffled advance of tanks, massing of supply trains just off the road, a general's touring car here and there — almost pushing everyone aside for the moment — we saw all this as we kept moving, hugging the one main road we knew would lead us right.

The barrage was to start at 1 o'clock and zero hour was 5 o'clock, so of course I knew we couldn't make the grade before the artillery opened. None of us had ever seen or heard the flash and thunder of the guns which tear down the enemy's wire and open the way for the infantry before, so you may imagine that I noted the approach of 1 o'clock with some misgiving.

The earth opened up. Man's cannon was competing with Nature's heaven in noise and light and rain. Powder explosion against thunder, artillery flash against lightning and shrapnel bullets against water were competing for first attention and it seemed to me that man acquitted himself quite creditably that morning.

If the earth opened up at 1 o'clock, the universe yawned at 5. The artillery gave them everything it had, the machine gun batteries started a barrage of their own, the airplanes went up, the trench mortars belched out a smoke screen and the tanks woke up.

Now that I look back, it's surprising how few casualties came to my immediate attention. There were no "rivers of blood," the trenches were not "filled with dead," our lines were not "mowed down like wheat," and the air was not filled with "moans of anguish from the mortally wounded." Of course, I have taken more peaceful strolls, but, to be plain about it, the boche I have seen do not want to fight. They will bombard, put over gas and stick to a machine gun, but when we really close in they throw up their hands and shout "kamarad."

The drive was over in two days and finally we dug in — we dug in in several places, or started to — and trench routine started again with its shelling and raiding and patroling and wiring and waiting for the relief which, it is rumored, always is coming tomorrow night.

OPERA IS 89TH'S TREAT

"O.P.H." Goes to Two Shows in One Night at the Front

At the First One, a Movie, a Spectator Falls Off a Stove — In the Jostle the Film Takes Fire, Ending Show.

(From The Star's Own Correspondent.)
WITH THE 89TH DIVISION, Dec. 1. — If you don't "kid" the war, the war will "kid" you. One of the best incidents of "kidding" the war I found in Bouillonville, fondly called "Souptown," headquarters of the All-Kansas regiment as well as the 353d and 355th Ambulance companies.

I found the boys having the time of their lives. The boche had once had an officers' club there, a recreation room for the soldiers and a large hospital. Therefore there was plenty to eat and drink. I had dinner with Capt. E.W. Cavaness, who organized the 355th Ambulance Company in Kansas City, and Capt. Christian H. Koontz of Onaga, Kas.

"A LITTLE PARTY TONIGHT."

Then I hunted up Sergt. Arthur Duncan, a former reporter on The Star, in the 353d Ambulance Company, which was raised at Fredonia, Hutchinson and Winfield. "Dunc" said the boys were "going to put on a little party tonight." So I stayed.

We had noticed a sign tacked on a door that read:

Moving Pictures Tonight, 8 O'clock. Admission 2 Cigarettes.

A few doors further down was another sign:

Patronize Your Allies. To Hell with the Boche. French Grand Opera Tonight. Admission 1 Cigarette.

We decided to take in both shows. At 8 o'clock we went to where the movie was to be held, and stood in line at the front door with our cigarettes in hand. Something evidently had hit the door, because there wasn't any door left. A gas blanket took its place. Inside was a sort of ante-

chamber, as dark as a stack of black cats. The "guest" had to pass through a second gas blanket, where he paid his fare and looked about for a seat on the floor of the smoke-filled little room.

IN THE SEAT OF HONOR.

The head usher gave me the seat of honor — the smooth CANside of an empty syrup can. Then he surreptitiously slipped me my two cigarettes, and whispered that while the house never made it a custom to issue any "comps," they would make an exception in my case and herewith returned the purchase price of my ticket, which I accepted, and returned half of it to him in exchange for a match. After which the candles were blown out and the show was ready to begin.

The picture machine was one of these small affairs that costs about $3 apiece at home. The pictures were thrown on a sheet stretched across the wall. The films were only about five feet long, fastened together in the shape of a belt, which worked on two wheels. Sergt. William Cunningham, better known as "Candy" Cunningham, was the operator. He formerly operated a movie of his own at Fredonia. Sergt. Leonard Sohn of Severy, Kas., was the official announcer. He stood beside the machine and explained the pictures.

The two evidently had rehearsed, because Sohn went right along with his speeches regardless of whether the machine was going. Sometimes he was ahead of the pictures, sometimes behind.

One film showed the kaiser and the kaiserin out for an airing. Sohn would run along like this:

"Now, ladies and gentlemen, you will see a life-size picture of the man whose dream it was to rule the world. He and his old lady will pass before you riding in a hack. There are three or four boobs scat-

92

tered around on different parts of the hack, but they haven't anything to do with the picture. Somebody just threw them in for good measure. Here they come now. The guy with the high hat sitting in the rear of the vehicle is Bill. The woman on his left is Mrs. Bill."

THE ANNOUNCER WAS FIRM.

The picture would be over and the lecturer would just be well started. But he had plenty of time because it took some time to adjust the machine for the next picture, and the lecture usually wouldn't be finished by that time. If it wasn't, the sergeant would put his hand over the projector and announce:

"These ladies and gentlemen have paid their good money to see this show, and they are going to see it all if I have anything to do with it."

Then he would continue until the lecture was ended.

"Dunc" had taken up a point of vantage on top of a little iron stove. Everybody was jammed in around him. Cunningham had thrown a picture on the screen showing the boche infantry in an attack. They were going forward at a great rate, mowing the Allied soldiers down before them. Then the stove was overturned, Duncan with it. Someone jarred the machine, causing the film to catch fire, and the show was over for the evening.

"Now we must go and listen to the grand opera," Duncan said.

"Do you think you can deadhead me in, because my cigarettes are running low," I asked him. He thought he could.

We wandered around until we came to what appeared like a black hole in the hillside. After more winding around we came to a curtain and there we were, right smack in the opera house.

"FIXED" THE MANAGEMENT.

I waited while Duncan "parlayed" with the "manager," Ernest Yount of Winfield, Kas. Duncan whispered in my ear that "everything had been squared with the management."

The hall was about as large as an ordinary living room. The place had been blasted out. Here and there candles were stuck into wine bottles. Sitting on a large box was the "grand opera," in the shape of a disc phonograph, being operated by Yount and Harry Evans of Kansas City, both motor mechanics. At first I couldn't quite understand why it needed motor mechanics to operate a phonograph, but I soon found out. In one place the boys had used the trachea tube of a gas mask to replace a part of the machine. The trachea tube is the rubber hose that connects the mouthpiece and the cannister on the gas mask, but just what it connected on the machine will always remain a mystery to me. In another place was a piece taken from a bicycle. In another place I found the handle from a razor blade sharpener.

"The next piece is 'The Cavalry Rushedthecan,'" the motor mechanic called out. "It is in French, and if you don't understand it, act like you do, because if you raise a rumpus the bounder will throw you out. Just remember that I've got two hand grenades in my pocket and I'll spatter you all over the wall. Proceed."

There it was, sure enough, "Cavalleria Rusticana," in the dulcet tone of a singer known to two continents. Someone had stepped on the record and cracked it a bit in the center, but we didn't notice that. Then followed the "Miserere," the Barcarole from "The Tales of Hoffman," the Soldiers' Chorus from "Faust," the jewel song from "Faust," the sextet from "Lucia" and others. It was worth the price.

A few hours later we went to bed in the office of the 353d Ambulance Company. "Dunc" rolled up alongside of me, while at my feet lay Herbert Roemer, a wholesale jeweler from Kansas City. Ray Holderman, who, before he joined the army, was piano instructor at the Winfield College of Music, had to sleep over by the window, because he was the telephone "girl" for that night and had to keep his head close to the telephone.   —O.P.H.

YANKS BATTLE IN RUSSIA
Advance Against Bolshevik Forces Made at Kadish.
Desperate Struggle Marked by Graves of Fallen Americans, Who Fought Under Great Handicaps — Enemy Mutilate Prisoners.

(By the Associated Press)
WITH THE ALLIED ARMY OF THE DVINA, Jan. 4 (delayed). — American troops, fighting desperately near Kadish, have driven back Bolshevist troops which made an advance there. The Bolshevists also launched attacked on the Onega sector and bombarded the Allied front. The Americans came into battle along the Petrograd road and in the frozen swamps that border it. The battle was fought in snow from two to four feet in depth.

The men engaged in the advance were from infantry and trench mortar units. This morning word came from headquarters that the American positions are now four hundred meters south of the village which is the line marking the furthest advance made by the Americans late in October, before they retired to the north of Kadish. Here and there are graves where are buried Americans who fell in the struggle that went on during the first advance. There are not many in number, but for the troops involved they give evidence that the Americans have been in the hardest fighting that has been going on here. The Bolshevists are fighting more savagely here than elsewhere to hold their positions.

ARE NEAR BOLSHEVIK BASE.

The Petrograd Road leads southward to Plesetakaya, a large village on the Volodga Railway, which is the enemy's base of operations with the Kadish and Onega fronts.

Allied positions on the Onega front near the village of Pechura were attacked by the enemy yesterday. This attack was centered on a Russian naval brigade, which held its positions, inflicting heavy losses without apparently losing a man. On the Volodga railway the Bolshevists have for the past three days kept up a strong artillery fire and have brought an armored train into action. Little damage apparently was done to Allied positions. On the other hand, an Allied shell struck an enemy barracks, doing great damage.

TROOPS ADVANCE ON SNOWSHOES.

In this sector Allied forces advanced on snowshoes over soft snow a few days ago. Beneath the snow was an unfrozen swamp, and the men often sank into the mud up to their waists in spite of their Arctic footgear. The battle with the elements makes the fighting here very difficult.

Further evidence that the Bolshevists are mutilating Allied wounded and dead came to headquarters today in a report from Lieutenant Colonel Corberly, who was in command of American forces in the vicinity of Shenkursk on November 29. Americans were the victims, according to the report. A patrol of sixty American soldiers and two officers was surprised early September 29 by a force of about seven hundred Bolshevists. Seven Americans were killed and seven others were missing after the fight. Following is the report of Lieutenant Colonel Corberly as to the condition of the bodies found after the engagements, the names of men being omitted:

"No. 1. Lieutenant, head smashed with ax.

"No. 2. Corporal, so smashed with ax that only part of the face remained.

"No. 3. Corporal, head smashed in with ax and arms and legs broken by blows, apparently from blunt side of ax.

"No. 4. Private, head smashed with ax.

"No. 5. Private, head smashed and throat cut open, apparently with ax."

The discovery of mutilated bodies at Shenkursk has brought a new spirit to the Americans, who are now fighting mad.

Today the fighting about Kadish apparently had ceased except for spasmodic artillery action.

TOWNS HELD BY THE 89TH
Kyllburg Is Headquarters — in Treves and Saarburg.

The Three Corps That Make Up the Third Army of Occupation Stretch from the Border Across the Rhine at Coblenz.

COBLENZ, Jan. 6 (by courier to Nancy). — The German territory held by the American 3d Army is much greater than is understood outside of military circles. The layman fancies the bridgehead shown on maps indicates a large part of the occupied ground, while it is really on the front line. As a matter of fact, with approximately the south third of the Coblenz bridgehead taken over by the French, the American occupied ground on the other side of the Rhine is only about one-eighth of the entire holding.

It is now permissible to give the official summary, location and employment of the three corps comprising this army. Hitherto it has been mentioned piecemeal, but with the official list from headquarters the folks back home will be able, at least roughly, to make their own maps showing how the American forces are spread out.

TERRITORY OF OUR ARMY.

The general location of the 3d Army with Major General Dickman in command, with headquarters in Coblenz, is described as Romage, Weroth, Coblenz, Berncastel, Rhaunen, Sierck and Ouren.

The list giving the location and other facts on the three army corps and constituent divisions follows: The 3d Corps, under General Hines, holds the bridgehead with headquarters at Neuwied and occupies Honningen, Herschbach, Putschbach and Coblenz. The 1st Division, under General McGlachin, is in the first line with headquarters at Montabaur and occupies Freilingen, Ruoschbach, Arzbach and Hohr. The 32d Division, under General Lassiter, is in the first line with headquarters at Rengsdorf, and occupies Breitscheid, Herschbach, Alsbach and Sayn. The 2d Division, under General LaJeune, is in support with headquarters at Heddendorf and occupies Rossbach, Arzheim and the right bank of the Rhine to Honningen.

THE 89TH A "SHOCK" UNIT
Returned Kansas City Man Tells of Argonne and St. Mihiel.
In Its First Heavy Action the Division Made Its 4-Day Objective in 42 Hours, J.W. McClintock, Back Wounded, Says.

NEW YORK, Jan. 7. — The story of the victories gained at St. Mihiel and in the Argonne by the 89th Division, the men from Kansas, Missouri and nearby states whose fighting abilities drew the division the envious position of "shock troops," was told today by a wounded member of the Funston contingent. He is J.W. McClintock, Kansas City, with Company C, 356th Infantry, until November 2, when bursting shrapnel incapacitated him in the fighting north of Romage, in the Argonne.

McClintock arrived in New York recently, going into United States Debarkation Hospital No. 3.

When the 89th Division first went into action at St. Mihiel September 12, McClintock's regiment was in front of Mont Sec, otherwise known as Hill 380, one of the strongest fortified positions in the German lines. French and British had sustained enormous losses in former attempts to take it. With the crack 1st and 2d Divisions on the left and right, respectively, the 89th was assigned a 12-mile objective, including the taking of the hill, four days being given in which to gain it.

The 89th went over the top at daybreak. Passing through a ruined village in what had been No Man's Land, the men took a woods beyond and at the foot of the hill. Tanks were used and the advance was made behind a 5-hour intensive barrage that had the Huns on the fortified hill sending up every form of S.O.S. flare they had.

TOOK THREE THOUSAND PRISONERS

The left side of the hill was stormed by the 1st Division, the 89th taking the right and making the top by 9 o'clock, after a sharp hour and a half attack. There some three thousand prisoners and more than one thousand horses, with many supplies, were captured. The 89th's casualties in the attack on Hill 380 were comparatively few, McClintock says, being probably not more than five hundred.

The first day's advance to Essy, Major Bland of the 89th was killed. McClintock describes the freak of shell fire responsible, being within a few yards of the spot at the time. The major was resting, surrounded by his staff, when shrapnel burst over them. By a strange chance Major Bland was picked off by one of the flying fragments, none of the others being touched.

WENT FIVE MILES WITH A RUSH.

That night the division "dug in" on a hillside at 6 o'clock. At 8 o'clock an order came to move forward, and an advance of five miles was made almost without opposition. At 4 in the morning the troops dug in once more and made a final advance to their objective at 8 o'clock. It is a notable fact that the 89th in this first heavy action made the 4-day objective in just forty-two hours. Once there, it dug in permanently and held until relieved against heavy attacking and shelling.

At one time on this front the entire division was subjected to fifty-five minutes of the most intensive shelling, with only a few casualties, through the fact an exceptionally heavy combat patrol was mistaken for a general attack. On returning after a night in No Man's Land it was found that one man was lost, and just at daybreak the patrol went out again to find him, with the result of the shelling by the frightened Germans. The lost man returned to the American trench late that afternoon, having become separated from the patrol and crawling all the way to the German wire before he found out that he was going in the wrong direction. There he had heard voices in German and had spent the rest of the night and almost all day in getting back.

THE FIGHTING IN THE ARGONNE.

The 89th Division went over the top on the day after it had arrived on the Argonne sector, advancing to Romage against stubborn resistance. In this attack it took the troops from the Middle West six days to go forward five miles. The division occupied Romage until November 1, when it again went over the top between the 1st and 2 divisions, advancing four miles. November 2 the 89th made one and one-half miles against heavy artillery resistance. This part of the advance was made under cover of what is described as the heaviest rolling barrage ever laid down to protect American troops.

It was here that McClintock left the division, being wounded by a fragment of German 77-M M. shell which killed two and wounded two others, all of whom were farther away from the explosion.

TRAPPED HUN MAP CARRIER.

In the advance in the Argonne, McClintock's company was featured in one of the most important captures made on the sector. Together with one platoon of B Company and a Stokes mortar platoon of Headquarters Company of the 356th, it had become lost in the Bois d Romain in heavy rain and mud. Taking possession of some deserted German billets, and trying to find out where they were, they heard a voice in German outside asking if it was the "5th Company." One of the men, who spoke German, answered that it was, and to come in. The man was captured and he proved to be a German artillery observation officer, carrying maps which disclosed the location of every gun emplacement for miles around. The men, who were in command of Lieut. J.P. Welch of Kansas City, were commended highly for the capture.

The men were surrounded in the Boise de Romain seventy-two hours without communication. After twenty-four hours they ran out of food and water, and with machine guns potting at them from all sides, they were in a bad way until they were located by an airplane. In holding their precarious position they killed and captured many Huns, and the relieving forces captured fifty machine guns, McClintock says, in getting to them.

MADE A "SHOCK" DIVISION.

The 89th Division, McClintock says, made such a good showing in its first action that it was designated for shock troops and placed between the crack 1st Division of infantry and the famous 2d Infantry and marines, the 2d being the unit that saved the day at Chateau Thierry.

McClintock also tells of the bravery of Major Hobson of the 356th in the action on the Toul sector in which he was wounded severely, but refused to stop. For his subsequent actions under heavy fire Hobson was awarded the Distinguished Service Cross.

Many men from the Middle West who were wounded in action with the 89th Division are in the debarkation hospitals in New York. They unite in giving credit to the training of General Wood at Camp Funston, together with the splendid personnel of the commissioned officers for the conspicuous showing made by the unit.

CITE MIDDLE WEST HEROES
Wounded, Men Refused To Quit Battle Against Huns.

Reports Describe Bravery of Kansas, Missouri and Nebraska Soldiers in Argonne, St. Mihiel and Other Actions.

WASHINGTON, Jan. 10. — First Lieut. Eilbert Heiken of Ottawa, Kas., with the 356th Infantry, 89th Division, has been cited for extraordinary heroism in action in the Argonne and St. Mihiel drives. The night of September 23, although wounded in the shoulder in the beginning of the attack on Domartin Wood, Lieutenant Heiken continued until his mission was accomplished successfully. The night of November 9, with eight men, he was the first to cross the Meuse and patrol enemy lines. The night of November 10, with twenty men, he covered the crossing of his battalion until he was wounded severely.

WOUNDED, FOUGHT TWO DAYS.

Sergt. Ralph M. Shimmeall of Norton, Kas., Company M, 353d Infantry, 89th Division, has been cited for extraordinary heroism near Bantheville, France. Sergeant Shimmeall, although wounded twice, continued in action two days without reporting for medical aid. He established and maintained liaison during those two days in a very efficient manner.

Other men included in the citations are:

Sergt. Elgin J. Moore, Oshkosh, Neb., Company C, 314th Signal Battalion, maintained lines of communication under shell fire.

Sergt. Roy M. Sauers, Fremont, Neb., Company B, 314th Field Signal Battalion. Over a road swept by shell fire he carried the line forward and kept it in constant repair.

Corp. Charles Lemasters, St. Paul, Neb., Company C, 314th Field Signal Battalion, maintained lines of communication under shell fire.

MISSOURIAN REFUSED TREATMENT.

Private Roy A. Bess, Glen Allen, Mo., Company L, 355th Infantry, wounded, refused first aid and continued in engagement two days without treatment.

Sergt. Lee B. McDaniel (deceased), Columbus, Kas., 353d Infantry, led his platoon with great bravery and coolness against cleverly concealed machine guns until he fell wounded severely.

Private John L. Dugan, Fort Scott, Kas., Company B, 353d Infantry, although wounded badly in the face, refused medical attention and assisted in attack on machine gun nest, capturing one gun himself.

INVITED DEATH TO INSPIRE MEN

Sergt. Otis V. Dozer, Cedarvale, Kas., Company F, 353d Infantry, fearlessly exposed himself in the face of machine gun fire to set example for his men. Wounded while advancing, he continued until exhausted. His coolness and courage resulted in the capture of three machine guns and their crews.

Pvt. Frank F. Tomanek, Quinter, Kas., Company I, 353d Infantry, volunteered to remain liaison with assault battalion in a heavy barrage, and carried out two such missions.

Pvt. Edward McGee, Tipton, Kas., Company M, 353d Infantry, volunteered to maintain liaison with assault battalion in shell fire, and carried out five such missions.

Sergt. Walter S. Witt, Paola, Kas., Company D, 353d Infantry, although wounded in the face, refused to go to the first aid station for treatment, remaining with platoon throughout engagement.

Pvt. William A. Hall (deceased), Winfield, Kas., Company A, 353d Infantry, acting as runner between his company and battalion headquarters, made several trips through severe artillery fire.

> Sergt. George W. Gardner, Traer, Kas., Company F, 353d Infantry, led a platoon through shell and machine gun fire in attack, capturing two machine guns and assisting in destruction of others holding up advance.

Private Andrew A. Benson, Bertrand, Neb., Medical Detachment, 1st Gas Regiment, although wounded severely, continued to give first aid until struck a second time, and then continued on duty.

Capt. Robert B. Hood, Hutchinson, Kas., Battery E., 12th Field Artillery, voluntarily left cover under terrific bombardment and carried wounded to safety.

CITE A SURGEON'S HEROISM

Asst. Surg. Frederick R. Hook, Rossville, Kas., United States Navy, attached to 5th Regiment Marines, established an advance dressing station under heavy fire, working fearlessly and unceasingly until ordered to retire.

Private Harry O. Westergren, Emporia, Kas., Headquarters Company, 5th Regiment, Marines, a runner, displayed exceptional courage in carrying messages over terrain constantly swept by machine gun and shell fire.

U.S. troops fighting in the Argonne Forest in the fall of 1918 faced fierce resistance. In six weeks, the American Expeditionary Forces lost 26,277 men (95,786 were wounded).

GENERAL WOOD TO CHICAGO
Charge of Central Department Given Funston Commander.
Orders Were Issued Today at Washington Directing the Transfer from Kansas Post — Succeeds General Barry.

WASHINGTON, Jan. 15. — Orders directing Maj. Gen. Leonard Wood, now commanding Camp Funston, Kas., to proceed to Chicago and take command of the Central Department were issued today by the War Department.

—

In taking command of the Central Department of the army, General Wood succeeds Maj. Gen. Thomas H. Barry, who goes to New York to the Department of the East, commanded until a few days ago by Maj. Gen. J. Franklin Bell, who died. General Wood, until the declaration of war, was in command of the Department of the East. He was then shifted to the newly created Department of the Southwest, and later was assigned to the command of Camp Funston and the 89th Division. On the eve of the 89th's departure overseas, General Wood was assigned to the Western Department at San Francisco. He asked to stay at Camp Funston and the orders were changed to give him command of the camp, but not of the 10th Division, being organized.

The Central Department comprises most of the Middle Western states, but the command does not carry with it command of Camp Funston, Camp Dodge, Ia., or Camp Grant, Ill. It does carry command of all of the forts, such as Fort Leavenworth, Fort Riley, Jefferson Barracks and Fort Sill.

New Central Department Commander.

From the latest photograph of Maj. Gen. Leonard Wood.

A GENERAL AND THEN A PRIVATE.
Red Cross Canteen Workers Didn't Turn the Page Quickly Enough.

The canteen workers of the Red Cross booth at the Union Station are always pleased when a soldier asks permission to write his name on the register they keep. Today they were exceptionally pleased when a soldier placed his name on a fresh page on the register. The solider was Maj. Gen. Leonard Wood. He just wrote his name: "Leonard Wood."

GENERAL WOOD HERE TODAY.
Time Will Be Divided Between Central Command and 10th Division.

Maj. Gen. Leonard Wood, who assumed command of the Central Department in Chicago yesterday afternoon, was in Kansas City this morning on his way to Camp Funston, where the demobilization of the Tenth Division will be continued. General Wood will remain at Camp Funston while the demobilization of the Tenth is in progress, going to his Chicago post only when necessary. When the division is no longer in the service, General Wood will make Chicago his permanent headquarters.

It is known that before finally accepting the command of the Central Department with headquarters at Chicago, General Wood asked that if the 10th Division remained in service he should continue in command of it or if it was to be demobilized he should remain with his division until demobilization was complete. The 10th is to be demobilized and the orders for General Wood's new command provided that he should divide his time between it and the 10th Division until the latter is out of service.

General Wood was returning from Oyster Bay, where he attended the funeral of his friend, Colonel Roosevelt, when the news of his appointment to the command of the Central Department reached him.

Gen. Douglas MacArthur, who commands a brigade of infantry with the Rainbow Division, nearly always gets out and leads his men in an attack. This means he is all up and down the brigade front, giving orders here, directions there, and dealing out encouragement and advice all the time. It is essential he have telephonic communication with the division and his regiments all the time.

In the fighting north of Exermont in the Argonne, Harry W.C. Oberg and Jake Hoffman, Kansas City linemen, had the job of following General MacArthur, keeping up a telephone connection for him. The two men strung two and one-half kilometers of wire behind the general in a heavy boche barrage, and then had to run all up and down the line keeping it in repair every time a shell knocked it out. It kept them mighty busy, and they had some narrow escapes. *— O.P.H.*

PLAN FOR FUTURE — WOOD
Lessons of Unpreparedness Must Not Be Lost
Camp Funston Commander Reviews Mistakes of Past and Urges Universal Military Training — Praise for Men of Middle West

In an address delivered without passion or prejudice, with criticism for no one for the mistakes made by this country because of its unpreparedness for the late war, but burning into the hears of his audience the necessity for universal military training as the only real safeguard for the Nation in the future, Maj. Gen. Leonard Wood at the Victory meeting of the Kansas City Bar Association at the Hotel Muehlebach last night, deeply impressed his hearers with the soundness of his doctrine.

Beginning with the Revolution and reciting all of the wars in which America has engaged, he told of the lessons taught by each and the good that resulted from them.

THE FUTURE TASKS.

"I simply desire to invite your attention to a few things which have been done and discuss a few which will come up later," said General Wood after his introduction by Ellison A. Neel, president of the bar association. "The war has been won and now, with the Allies, we are discussing peace. I do not think that our late enemy will haggle much over the terms.

"All of our men that got into the fight gave a good account of themselves. You of the Middle West should feel proud of the 89th and the 35th divisions. While I saw little of the 35th, I do know something of the 89th. There is no question about their service. The last letter I had from the chief of staff told me that the 89th had taken 4,000 boche prisoners and lost practically none. They were in the Argonne Forest after that, however, so I do not know what happened there, but I know that they acquitted themselves like the men they are.

NOT THE LAST WAR.

"This is the end of the present war, but I do not believe there are any so Utopian as to believe that this is the last war. When we entered this war, we had to build from the ground. You will recall, those of you who came to Camp Funston, how you saw the first contingents of the National Army in overalls and blouses, the infantry drilling with wooden guns, many of which the men carved out with their pocket knives; you saw the artillery drilling with cannon made from telegraph poles. Germany knew of this and naturally underestimated our strength. With this beginning, however, you know what progress was made — slow at the beginning, but how it grew, and grew, and grew.

"In telling of our achievements across the water do not underestimate the splendid valor of our men; give them full credit, but do not say 'We won the war' for we did not. We came in late, very late, but we got busy and made a showing after we did get in.

NO AIRPLANE THERE.

"If we take the report of Mr. Hughes, recently published, and there is no reason to doubt it, our airplanes had not reached the front when the armistice was signed. A few bombing planes were there, the report says, but none of the scout variety.

Big things like preparing for war cannot be accomplished overnight. If the Hun had struck us, unprepared, we would have had plenty of willing souls and strong bodies but without arms or training. We had five thousand regular officers at the beginning of the war, 3,700 of them line officers, the rest on the staffs. This had to be increased to over two hundred thousand officers and it had to be done almost over night.

NATIONAL HABIT OF MIND.

"Men were put through intensive training and made officers in three months. It should require six months to equip an officer for duty. And officers had to be picked from these new men to train others. That is the condition in which war found us, but should not find us again. The condition is not charged to any party or to any group of men. It was simply a condition of national habit of mind. And this was due largely to the teaching in our schools.

"We won the war of the Revolution because France came to our aid with a division of trained men just in time to turn the tide. And, thank God, we have had a chance to pay the interest on that debt."

ARMY BEST FOR WAR.

Here the general went into a history of the Revolution and said the best history of that war is found in the letters of Washington. He quoted from those, "The best way to have peace is in a good army," and, "In time of peace prepare for war."

"You will observe," said the speaker, "Washington did not say 'against war' but 'for war.' "

PREPARED FOR MEXICAN WAR.

General Wood quoted Jefferson and Adams on preparedness and followed by a review of the condition of the country in subsequent wars. He said that the best army was found in the Mexican War of 1848 where the men, all crack shots with a rifle, "were trained far from home and without interference." He referred to the fact that the Allies, "our associates," as he called them, gave us time in the present war to equip and train our men without any danger to them or the country.

ON PAST PREDICTIONS.

"The Spanish-American War was a little war," he went on. "It was with a country inferior in strength to our own — but," he added with a smile, "its fleet came out and fought, it did not surrender.

"Then came this great struggle. Many listened to the statement of Sumner in 1848 that there never would be another great war. Others talked of how easily we could raise a million men over night. There is nothing more dangerous than the statement, 'There will be no more wars.' Go into the Balkans where most all the trouble of late years has originated and see if you can convince yourself that there will be no more wars.

"Like the French we should live a national life conscious of no wrong and conscious of no fear."

A "FINE OUTFIT" IS 89TH

Comrades Praise Kansas and Missouri Division.

Major General Wood Is Lauded by a War Writer for His Part in Training Middle States Fighters.

The 89th Division, "our division," composed almost exclusively of Kansans and Missourians, and trained by Major General Wood at Camp Funston, has the reputation of being a "fine outfit" among fighters in Europe. Since its dispatch to France last March, the 89th has been in almost every major engagement in which the Americans have participated. The tribute paid the men from the Middle West by their comrades is described as follows by Damon Runyon, now with the army of occupation, in the Chicago Herald and Examiner:

One of the favorite sports on the Rhine these days is the rating or, rather, the attempted rating, of different combat divisions, much after the fashion which sporting writers used to rate football teams at the close of a season.

Which was the greatest division and which did the most notable work are questions that probably will be argued down through the ages, especially by members of the different fighting outfits — with but small chance they'll ever agree.

Every soldier proudly maintains that his organization is the finest, and no one will ever be able to change that opinion.

And while unanimity on any one phrase of the discussion is difficult to obtain, there is a proposition on which there seems to be pretty general agreement.

It is that one of the best of the national army or draft divisions, if not indeed the very best, is the 89th.

When the 89th is mentioned, both regular Army men and National Guardsmen nod their heads and say: "It's a fine outfit." They don't admit that it is better than their own, but they agree upon its merits without cavil.

IN LINE AT THE FINISH.

And now see how the 89th is grist in the mills of the gods that are said to grind with such exceeding fineness. It was sent to the war by Gen. Leonard Wood, no less. He started for France at the head of the division, but was forced to turn back. That was a bitter blow to him, but he ought to find some consolation in the record of his division.

It fought from St. Mihiel to the Meuse. It was credited with one of the most important operations of the last drive. It was in line at the finish. Finally it was chosen among the American divisions sent to the Rhine.

The 89th was trained by General Wood at Camp Funston, in Kansas. It is made up of an all-Missouri and an all-Kansas regiment, with a scattering of members from Nebraska, New Mexico, Colorado, the Middle Western and the Rocky Mountain states.

THE PART OF A LONELY SOLDIER.

You can tell a member of the 89th a block away by his shape and military bearing.

—

"New England troops formed the spearhead that broke the German war machine," says the Boston Globe. And similar statements in behalf of the boys from other sections can be found in every paper from Tampa to Seattle, and Los Angeles to Bangor. But shucks! Everybody knows, if he'd admit it, that it was the 35th and the 89th divisions who won the war.

WHEN 89TH HEARD NEWS
An Intercepted Radiogram Told of Germany's Surrender.
Kansas and Kansas City Men Were Taking Boche Prisoners
Less Than an Hour Before War Ended, "O.P.H." Writes

(By Cable from The Star's Own Correspondent.)

WITH THE 89TH DIVISION IN FRANCE, Nov. 11 (delayed). — That the Germans had accepted all armistice terms was known in the intelligence section of the 89th Division at 9 o'clock last night. Information was picked up from a German radiogram and was translated at that hour, but those who knew were sworn to absolute secrecy until the official announcement.

There were Capt. Ingram Hook, a Kansas City officer formerly with the 356th Infantry, later an instructor in the third officers' training camp at Camp Funston, now an operations officer of the division; Maj. Frank Wilbur, Smith, an assistant chief of staff, and myself.

THEN CAME THE BIG NEWS.

An orderly from headquarters walked into the room where we sat. He had a copy of a German radiogram intercepted, in the original German tongue and code.

Translated, it read:

"Accepted all armistice terms."

Everybody yelled. Everyone was sworn to secrecy until the official word came from headquarters. Next morning we obtained a motor car and went to the east bank of the Meuse,

We told the artillery headquarters of the intercepted radiogram saying the armistice was signed. The commanding officer said: "Continue firing until the targets supplied are finished."

A message came from headquarters.

"Stop firing at 11 o'clock. Keep your eyes open and watch enemy. Do not fraternize with him," it read.

The shell-torn buildings rang with cheers.

"The war's over," they yelled.

That was back in the section held by the artillery and by the division headquarters.

With three other correspondents I jumped into the motor car to race to the front to witness the cessation of the great war.

We stopped a truck train filled with shells and told the men.

DIDN'T BELIEVE THE REPORT.

They did not believe us and looked at us with suspicion, as though fearing we might be traitors or tricksters.

We passed a company of doughboys, going to relieve fighting troops.

"The war is over," I shouted to them.

Their only reply was astonished queries as to what I was talking about.

"An armistice has been signed and all fighting will stop," I continued.

"What time does that peace begin?" one asked me. It then was 10 o'clock.

"Eleven o'clock, I answered, and there was a hasty glancing at watched.

Thy cheered and then they were sober.

"There's an hour yet," a sergeant yelled. "Come on, let's hurry." Away they went on their hike, evidently trying to get to the front before it was too late.

THE WOUNDED WERE SKEPTICAL.

We overtook an ambulance filled with wounded men. Leaning near, I yelled the good news.

"Cut the comedy," was the responde.

More doughboys and again we told the story.

"Take my gun," one answered and shoved it at me. "I don't want the thing any more."

Another bunch threw their helmets away and danced and sang.

The roads were covered with dead horses and a few dead men. Much enemy material was lying near.

As we passed through Beauclair and La Neuville, the enemy stopped shelling those places. Coming to the river, we found it at flood stage and the approaches destroyed. Crawling on logs and rocks and hanging to trees and vines, we were able to reach the bridge and cross into Stenay.

There we found many Kansas and Kansas City men. Patrols from the 353d Regiment were in the town, and the entire regiment came in within a half hour. Some of the boches still were in the city.

We were standing by a deserted building when we saw two Kansas men rush into it and bring out three boches.

The evening of November 10th when they arrived from the Argonne Forest from fighting, they went into a barn to sleep on hay. Early the next morning, a soldier came in and shouted, "The war is over! The war is over!" One of the soldiers rose up and said, "Why the hell don't you get out of here!"

YANKS DID A GOOD "JOB"
Marshal Foch Commends American Efficiency and Bravery.
The 1st. 2d and Rainbow Divisions Were the First,
but a Score of Others Got into Victory Drive.

By Junius B. Wood.
(Special Cable to The Chicago Daily News.)

WITH THE AMERICAN ARMY IN FRANCE, Nov. 16. — Marshal Foch's felicitation to General Pershing on the efficiency of the American general staff and the valor of the fighting men was the most valued endorsement possible of America's part in the final victory. The supreme commander of the Allied forces has spoken frankly and sincerely, like a soldier. Coming at the present time, when peace has come and the Allies are confronted with new problems, the endorsement has deep significance.

It cannot be too strongly impressed upon the public that the American fighting men have done most valuable work in winning the war. In addition to the part played by the 1st and 2d armies, other American units have taken gallant parts with the French, British, Belgian and Italian armies, as well as with the British and Japanese troops in Russia. General Pershing's offer to throw in the American troops wherever Marshal Foch deemed it necessary was taken advantage of continuously. The French also put in a certain number of their own divisions under the command of the Americans, but there were not considerable.

A GREAT FORCE IN BELGIUM.

European newspapers in connection with the latest Belgian activities in Flanders mentioned Americans as assisting. Military reasons have made it inadvisable to disclose the exact figures, but these may be roughly indicated by the statement that the Belgian fighting force was composed of rather more than three Americans to four Belgians.

The Americans in the French, British and Italian armies were considerably smaller in proportion to the total strength of the nations. However, in these days when the fighting strength of armies is computed by millions of men, it may be said that the fighting strength of the Americans in Europe was not far from half of that of the French and British combined.

BORE THEIR FULL SHARE.

One thing certainly stands out. When American divisions were included in the French and British armies, they invariably received their full share of the fighting against the enemy. Time after time these fresh young soldiers from across the Atlantic were either the driving wedge in the Allied attacks or the anchor around which the others rallied to withstand the German onslaughts. In either case they acquitted themselves nobly of the task.

Battles in which the Americans took part follow:

Battle at Montdidier, April 26; 1st Division.

Battle at Cantigny, May 30; 1st Division.

Battle at Le Thillot Famre, June 2; 2d Division.

Battles at Beleau Woods, Vaux and Torcy, June 5; 2d Division. On the same day the 2d and 28th divisions helped the French hold the Germans at the bridgehead of Chateau Thierry on the west bank of the Marne. The engagement was continuous, and Chateau Thierry fell to the French and Americans July 21.

Battle at Chalons-sur-Marne, beginning July 15; 42d (Rainbow) Division and the 93d Division, with French, British and Italian units.

Battle at Soissons, the beginning of the great Allied offensive, July 18. On this day

An unusual profile view of Ferdinand Foch, Marshal of France and Generalissimo of the Allied Forces.

the drive was renewed on Chateau-Thierry, which was taken July 21.

Before the Aisne was reached in this drive, the 3d, 4th, 26th, 42d and 77th American divisions had taken part.

Battles at Hamel and Albert, August 21; 33d Division.

Battle at Canal du Nord, September 4; 27th and 30th divisions.

The St. Mihiel offensive, September 12; 1st, 2d, 26th, 42d and 89th divisions.

Battle north of Chatons, October 3; 2d Division.

Advance on Lille, October 7, 42d Division, with the British.

MANY WERE IN LAST DRIVE.

The rest came in the last offensive when the Americans were given the toughest spot on the entire line between Switzerland and the North Sea — the hinge position pivoting on Verdun and swinging from the Meuser to the Aisne. The 33d, 18th, 4th, 79th, 37th, 91st, 35th, 28th and 77th divisions made the initial attack on September 26 with the 3d, 32d and 92d divisions in support. Later in the days of fighting the 1st, 5th, 26th, 29th, 42d, 78th, 82d and 90th divisions took their places in the line.

In the midst of all this some of the divisions and other new divisions were transformed to the 2d Army which had been formed.

When Dad was in Germany with the Army of Occupation for a year, there was a German lady who would cook for some of the army men. They would save sugar from wherever they ate and give it to her, and she would make a cake. When the war ended and the army troops were headed for the U.S., she cried, because she had better food when they were there.

THE 353RD INFANTRY GOES OVER THE TOP IN ST. MIHIEL OFFENSIVE — THE SECOND BATTALION MAKES THE ASSAULT

It is freely admitted that the outcome of a modern military offensive is largely dependent upon the physical condition, intelligence and morale of the individual soldiers engaged. And yet the magnitude and complexity of movement and forces is such that there is little left for him but to "do and die" or perhaps as the Americans put it, "do or die."

For more than a month the 353rd Infantry had been at the front in the Lucey sector on the southern leg of the St. Mihiel salient. Each battalion had taken its turn in the outguard, support and reserve positions. September 11, 1918, found the First Battalion for the second time on the outguard line. The Second Battalion had been redoubling its efforts to get ready for the assault and was now in the support positions. The Third Battalion was in reserve in the De Merve Woods. Each day had brought increasing signs of "something doin' " in the near future. The Second Division had established headquarters in Manonville and were taking positions on the right. Big guns were being pulled into place day and night; reconnaissance parties of other organizations were carefully moving about the sector. From the jumpiness and activity of his artillery and the searching expeditions of his aircraft, Fritz must also have sensed something unusual on the American side, but "D" Day found the officers and men of the 353rd Infantry almost unaware of the specific part they were to play in the great offensive of September 12.

Four long years the enemy had held the ground in St. Mihiel salient which the Crown Prince had won in his futile effort to take Verdun. During these years, the German High Command had done its best to make the positions secure by improving the natural advantages of the terrain with many strands of barbed wire entanglements of every description and various types of field fortifications. For, by holding this salient whose line extended approximately forty miles with its apex at the town of St. Mihiel on the Meuse, the Germans could still threaten Verdun and prevent traffic over the railroad from Verdun to Nancy — a main line of lateral communication with the French forces on the left. To reduce St. Mihiel salient was the immediate objective of the first all-American offensive under the personal command of General Pershing. It must be remembered in this connection that General Pershing had insisted from the first upon a distinctive American army. But up to this time emergencies in the allied operations made it necessary to throw American divisions into the line to check what the Germans had been pleased to call their great "Victory Drive." Cantigny and Chateau Thierry were, therefore, the forerunners of this first independent American operation which had been planned a year before.

At about the same time, this propaganda for the benefit of the German troops at the front was picked up:

"Men have always gone to war for ideals, have fought solely for honorable principles, with hatred and clenched teeth, but the Americans have entered the war for sport. Their chivalry has become so debased that they fight for trophies and offer prizes for killing the largest number of German soldiers."

In order to prevent any possible "leak" to the enemy, all information as to the plans of the drive was kept secret to the last moment. It was rumored that the German already had listened in on telephone communications within the sector, so caution was perhaps over-emphasized. Not until the evening of September 11th was Colonel Reeves able to give final directions to his battalion commanders, who then gave instructions to company commanders, and company commanders in turn gave instructions to platoon commanders.

In the plan of battle, the 353rd Infantry was to drive through the enemy positions to the right of Mort Marc Woods. The Second Battalion formed in two echelons with Companies "E" and "F" in advance, supported by Companies "G" and "H" at a distance of five hundred meters made the assault. The Third Battalion similarly deployed in depth was in sport. Companies "B," "C" and "D" of the First Battalion were to guard the left flank of leading waves and to mop up Mort Marc Woods as the advance continued, while Company "A" was to form combat liaison with the Second Division on the right. The Regimental M.G. Company accompanied the assault battalion. When the objectives of the first day had been reached, the Third Battalion was to leap-frog the Second Battalion and carry on to the final objective of the big offensive, with the first in support and the second in reserve.

The plan itself was very simple in its conception. But it must be remembered that no man in the 353rd Infantry was familiar with the ground. To make matters even worse, maps and compasses were scarce. At dusk the different outfits began to move to their jumping-off places. The roads were crowded with men. In the darkness some groups lost contact with their own outfits and were delayed in teaching their positions. Reliefs were only partially carried out. It was a dark night; a cold rain was falling — now a drizzle, now a downpour; the bottom of the tenches held water ankle deep. This was the situation during the night of September 11th.

The Second Battalion, scheduled to make the assault on the following morning, moved during the night from the support positions along St. Jean-Noviant road to the jump-off line out in "No Man's Land." There crouched down in the mud-filled trenches with thousands of fellow Americans, we waited for the Zero hour. All surplus clothing except raincoats had been stored and it seemed that Zero was upon us while we shivered and waited for the hour. Officers, non-commissioned officers and runners continued to be busy. In fact, there seemed to be plenty for everyone to do. It was impossible to remember all the instructions. One warning, however, stuck fast — "No one goes to the rear." Final orders read:

> "In a battle there is no time to inquire into the identity or motives of persons who create panic, disorganization or surrender. It is the duty of every officer and soldier to kill on the spot any person who in a fight urges or advises anyone to surrender or to stop fighting. It makes no difference whether the person is a stranger or a friend, or whether he is an officer or a private."
> (G.O. No. 5, Headquarters Fourth Army Corps; A.E.F., September 6, 1981.)

So we waited for the time to go "Over the Top."

At exactly one o'clock the preparatory bombardment began. More than a million rounds of ammunition were consumed in the artillery preparation which lasted from 1 a.m. to 5 a.m. All along the line the sky was lit up with flashes of heavy-caliber guns, distributed in depth for almost ten kilometers to the rear. In the intermissions between deafening explosions could be heard the puttering of machine guns. Very-lights and rockets of many colors went up from the enemy lines, then came into view a new kind of fireworks — a big ball of fire that seemed to explode in midair, fell to the ground, and glided along as if on wheels. It was a sight that fascinated the eyes. At first the sensibilities seemed to be numbed and then electrified. Thus, after four years of comparative inactivity, our "quiet" sector had come into its own with a vengeance.

There was practically no counter-bombardment of our positions. This unexpected good fortune permitted us to continue final preparations for the jump-off. Small detachments from the 314th Engineers assisted us in cutting our way through the wire, and clearing trenches of obstacles. As early as 4 a.m. groups began to steal forward until the entire battalion had formed up only a hundred yards or so from the first German trench. Units were closed up as much as possible, to escape the expected counter-barrage. At 5 o'clock an almost solid wall of fire swooped down upon the enemy front line trench — our barrage had begun. After twenty minutes it began to roll back, as it swept slowly across the German trench system, combat units of the Second Battalion, with wide intervals and distances, began to advance, following the barrage almost too closely. At this critical moment word came that Major Wood was disabled and Captain Peatross assumed command of the battalion.

The enemy's elaborate bands of wire in front of his position had been little cut by the preliminary bombardment, and only by energetically trampling and tearing our way through it could the battalion advance. The enemy had made the mistake of matting it so closely in some places that the determined, big-footed doughboys were able to run over the top. In other places it had to be cut or blown up with benglor torpedoes. The men lost no time but threw off raincoats and drove ahead.

Our barrage had completely demoralized the scattering outposts and practically no resistance was met in crossing the Ansoncourt line of trenches. But as the advance companies approached Robert Menil trench, they met deadly machine gun fire from the Euvezin Wood. The next half kilometer, from this trench to within the woods was one of bitter fighting. German machine gunners claimed a heavy toll. Check in Company "F" totaled nine killed and twenty-seven wounded. In Company "G" Lieutenant Wray had fallen, mortally wounded at a hundred yards beyond the jump-off line. Stretcher Bearers Holmes and Lamson of his company had given up their lives in an effort to reach him. Captain Adkins, so severely wounded that he had to be helped along, kept forward in command of his company for almost six kilometers until he was carried from the field near Thiacourt. First Sergeant West was found with his rifle to his shoulder, his head dropped forward. A bullet-hole through his helmet told the story. Without regard to losses the men fought on until the last German gunners were killed. "He's done everything he could do, now it's up to him to pay the price," reasoned the men as they mopped up the trenches to the last man.

Some losses occurred, too, from our own artillery. "Follow the barrage," were the orders. As soon as the barrage had lifted from an objective ahead the men moved up, not realizing that the artillery would roll back almost to their own position before moving forward again to the next objective. As a result, Lieutenant Shaw was the victim of one of our own shells a minute after he had led his platoon out, but his example carried the men forward without their commander and in spite of many losses. While Lieutenant Wickersham was advancing with his platoon a shell burst at his feet and threw him into the air with four mortal wounds. He dressed the wounds of his orderly, improvised a tourniquet for his own thigh and then ordered the advance to continue. Although weakened by the loss of blood, he moved on with his pistol in his left hand until he fell and died before aid could be administered to him. Everywhere action was heroic. Resistance and difficulties only brought it into the sublime.

Eagerness of the men to get forward in spite of the delay due to the machine gun resistance led to the serious error of telescoping on the part of the supporting units. Company "H" had pushed up to the right of Company "F" and Company "G" to the left of Company "E" and the Third Battalion had come to within a few meters of our assaulting line. The Divisional Airmen swept low over the advancing troops, waving and shouting at them to scatter. However, the aggressiveness of the assault had had its effect upon the enemy. Resistance weakened at the edge of the woods. A few snipers up in the trees continued to cause casualties, but American marksmanship was proof against such tactics. As soon as a treeman revealed his position, the crack of a rifle brought him tumbling like a squirrel to the ground. In the woods, the men fell irresistibly into skirmish line and dashed on through the thick underbrush. When Colonel Reeves asked a small party of stranded marines what they were doing in the rear of our men, they replied, "Tryin' to keep up with them d—— corn huskers."

Out into the triangular open space between the Euvezin Wood and the Beau Vallon Wood, combat units began to reform. Some machine gun resistance developed on the left flank, but was quickly overcome. The right was held up for a few moments by a heavy machine gun implacement, until Sergeant Moore of company "F" succeeded in gaining possession of one of the guns and turning it on the rest of the nest. The Vallon trench was not organized and the enemy was in rapid retreat throughout the sector. The Third Battalion was to pass the lines of the Second and take up the assault beyond the Vallon trench, which was designated as the third objective. Some of the units had already entered the Beau Vallon Wood. Colonel Reeves was on the ground. Realizing the confusion incident to a passage of the lines in the timber, and fearing that in some cases the third objective had not been fully developed, he promptly ordered the Second Battalion to continue the assault until the fourth objective, just beyond the Wood. Here the passages of lines was made.

For five kilometers through the elaborate trench system and the intricate wire entanglements of the enemy, through the densely intertwined undergrowth of the woods, the men of the Second Battalion had carried the assault. They had overcome desperate machine gun defenses, and braved the explosion of shells in their midst. Four hours and forty-five minutes the advance continued. Three officers and nearly two hundred men were wounded. Four officers and thirty-five enlisted men had made the supreme sacrifice.

BACK TO THE LINE IN THE BENEY SUBSECTOR, SUICIDE WOODS. THE SECOND BATTALION ON THE OUTGUARD

Almost before the battalions had halted on their way back to the positions as Divisional Reserve, orders came to relieve the 356th Infantry in the Beney subsector. We were "out o' luck" again. This new position was just to the left of the one previously occupied in the vicinity of Xammes. Company commanders and platoon sergeants dragged themselves wearily back to the front line on the night of September 19th. At the very time of the reconnaissance the Germans attempted a raid on the 42nd Division (Rainbow) occupying the sector to the left. As a consequence the reconnoitering parties received a hard shelling as a welcome. The first impressions of this sector were, therefore, anything but favorable.

Fortunately, the relief was postponed for twenty-four hours and we were given another day to clean up and replace shortages of essential equipment. Even in this position on the southern edge of Beau Vallon woods we had not escaped the shelling of Fritz's long-range guns. There was considerable speculation about the location of these guns that followed us with their devilish H.E. shells. Rumor had it that we were receiving fire from the fortifications around Metz, but this was only one of the many rumors. The situation of most concern was the return to the front line where Fritz registered so many direct hits.

On the night of September 21-22 after a march of more than twelve kilometers over muddy roads, carrying heavy packs and new supplies of ammunition, the Second Battalion again entered the outguard line. Just before entering the open space between Xammes Woods and Dampvitoux Woods the battalion had been held up by vigorous shelling, but the relief was effected in good time without casualties. Our outposts extended from the broad gauge railroad track on the left where we had a liaison group with the famous Shamrock Battalion of the Rainbow Division, along the northern edge of Charey Woods, across the low open ridge to about a kilometer east of the northern tip of Xammes Woods where we connected up with the outposts of the 354th Infantry. The companies on the outguard line from left to right were: "G," "E" and "H." "F" Company was in support in the northern edge of Dampvitoux Woods. During the day time troops in the open meadow drew back to alternative positions in the Xammes Woods. The First Battalion was in support, back farther in the Dampvitoux Woods. The Third Battalion was in reserve immediately west of Beney. Regimental Headquarters were established within the confines of this shell-frequented little town. The rear echelon remained in Bouillonville. Thus the men of the 353rd Infantry again found themselves actively opposed to the enemy.

THE FIRST BATTALION MOPS UP MARE WOODS ON THE LEFT FLANK OF THE REGIMENTAL SECTOR AND FORMS LIAISON WITH SECOND DIVISION ON THE RIGHT FLANK.

From the first day on the front line in the Lucey sector, men of the 353rd Infantry had faced Mort Mare Woods. For two and one-half kilometers its ragged edge extended beyond our advanced positions. On the map its boundaries were well defined, but as it actually stretched out before our eyes, it showed uncertain limits lost in the brush that had grown up since the beginning of the war. Many of the old trees were scarred and disfigured by the fragments of high explosive shells. Intelligence reports contained information as follows:

"Area eight square kilometers, wire has been put all through Mort Mare Woods and is about one meter high and varies in depth. This wire is strung from tree to tree and does not follow any regular line. In addition to the communicating trenches which lead to the rear, there is evidence that the edges of the fort openings through Mort Mare Woods have been prepared for flank defense. It is probably that anti-tank guns are in position to defend these passages. Batteries are scattered through the woods and also in the opening cut between the woods and the second position. Machine gunners are known to be located —" (Here followed a long table of co-ordinates.).

But to the doughboys, Mort Mare remained a patch of green woods covering a mystery, until September 12. Of one thing we were sure, it was occupied by the enemy. Men on duty in listening posts had heard the Germans at their work. Captain Dahmke's one-pounder had knocked some observers out of a tree. Patrols had already drawn the fire of its machine gunners, and there was no question but that its foliage made up the camouflage for many big guns. But just what was there no one knew until the morning of the big offensive, when Companies "B" and "D" of the First Battalion advancing on the left flank of the assaulting waves until well within the enemy positions, turned to the left to mop up Mort Mare Woods. (Company "C" continued on with the assaulting battalion to mop up Euvezin Woods, while Company "A" formed combat liaison with the Second Division.). It was what Colonel Reeves characterized in his report on the St. Mihiel offensive, "A very delicate mission, one difficult to execute." In fact, the commander of the Second Division anticipated serious difficulty from this quarter and placed an extra battalion on his left flank for any emergency.

The First Battalion was holding the outguard line at the time of the offensive. Only five days before, Company "D" had repulsed the determined raid of the Germans at the cost of three dead and seven wounded. Our companies had not been relieved and on the morning of the 12th were still widely scattered. Under these conditions Mort Mare Woods was easily translated "Sea of Death" for the First Battalion.

Captain Wood (commanding Company "D"), in a personal account gives some details of the circumstances under which the duty had to be performed:

"I received a message September 11 to report to Battalion Headquarters. Arriving there I found the other company commanders already assembled. The battalion commander, Captain Crump, was at Regimental Headquarters for final instructions. When he returned at about five o'clock in the afternoon, we held a conference in which we went over our orders for the drive to take place the following morning.

"With the platoons widely separated, the short time left, with the continuous shelling, the problem of holding a conference with the platoon commanders when I returned to my own P.C. was rather difficult. Finally, at eight o'clock, the four platoon commanders with Lieutenant Hunter and myself assembled to discuss the plans of the attack. Our mission was, after reaching the second objective, to turn to the left and mop up Mort Mare Woods."

ON THE WAY TO THE MEUSE-ARGONNE OFFENSIVE

The transition from the Pannes-Flirey-Limey sector to the scene of the Meuse-Argonne offensive falls readily into three phases. The first phase concerns the relief from the old sector. Division Field Order Number 29, dated 4 a.m., October 6, 1918, stated:

> "This division will move to and occupy area Bouconville-Bernecourt-Royaumeiz-Boucq (Exclusive)—Corneiville."

Billeting details had left the sector ahead of time for the new area. Their destination was unknown, but all indications pointed to replacements and a period of recuperation for the 89th Division.

Troops of the 37th Division were a day late in making the relief, and there was some uncertainty about transportation. The Second Battalion, however, was fortunate enough to secure truck transportation which carried the men in good shape to Jouy by 1 a.m., October 9th. The First and Third Battalions were left to make their way out on foot. The First Battalion arrived in Jouy about noon of October 9th. The Third Battalion landed in Corneiville on the same day.

Lieutenant Gallenkamp, the historian of the Third Battalion, gives a vivid account of the Third Battalion's march from St. Benoit to Corneiville.

> "At 4:45 it seemed that we were doomed to failure. Every bit of the trench was jammed, making lateral movements very difficult, so I crawled on top and tried to collect my men. It soon became apparent that if we went on time I would have to go with one platoon and trust to getting the company together later. I had great confidence in Lieutenant Jones and the other platoon leaders. At five o'clock the whole mass jumped out of the trench and started through the wire. The first man to be killed in my vicinity was Private Reyelts of "D" Company. He was hit by a rifle bullet just as he jumped out of the trench. I became entangled in the wire and had my leggins completely torn off. On the way across we came in contact with Lieutenant Jones' platoon. I now had half of my company together. At the foot of the hill I looked back and saw the most inspiring sight of my life. Streaks of light were breaking over the hill tops, leaving a silver background for the thousands of advancing American soldiers silhouetted on the horizon. Each stern face showed determination to mix it up with the enemy.
> "For the first hundred yards we met with little resistance, then the line was held up. I went forward and saw one man lying in the trench shot through the leg. Another was lying behind a bush receiving first aid. I started to cross to where they were when machine gun bullets tore up the ground near my feet. In the timber to the left, a path was cut through the brush to a big tree where the gunners were located. I started a squad to flank them out but they reported back that they could not get through. Lieutenant Metzger then took a few men around to the left and drove them out, but they got away. About the same time,

Mechanic Hanlin spotted a sniper in the same tree. With one well-placed shot he brought him down dead. Hanlin, poor fellow, was killed later in the day.

"We took advantage of the cover afforded by a ridge which we had now reached to re-organize the company, and then started to advance through the timber, but the company had split again. I lost contact with the platoon on the right and did not see them again until the next morning. While they were not with us, they did their part in an excellent manner. The mix-up was quite general. I gained an entire platoon from Company "C" when Lieutenant Lewis reported to me that he was lost.

"No sooner had the men entered the woods when there were cries of 'Kamerad' and the Boche began coming out with hands in the air. They seemed rather stupefied as a result of the terrific bombardment of our artillery. We lined them up in column of two's and sent them back with a very small guard. The prisoners carried the wounded, both Americans and Germans. A German officer refused to help carry a litter, but after receiving about an inch of a bayonet he decided to obey. These are only small incidents of the work in hand."

After the first determined resistance of the enemy had been overcome, the men of the Second Battalion found their most serious difficult in getting through the underbrush. There were plenty of narrow lanes, and in some places these were covered with corduroy walks, but all of these were carefully avoided as machine gun traps. The main business on hand was to rout the Germans out of their dugouts where they had sought protection from the bombardment, and start them to the rear. A shout down the entrance usually brought forth a bunch with their hands over their heads. If answer failed, down went a grenade to make sure that we were leaving no enemies to the rear. When the grenade had done its work the doughboy with his bayonet at "guard" made his way down the narrow passage. He must make assurance doubly sure, abut above all he must satisfy his curiosity.

WITH REGIMENTAL HEADQUARTERS AND
THE FIRST BATTALION IN MANOIS

The arrival at Manois gave the soldiers their first opportunity for studying a typical French village. This one lay almost in the center of Haute Marne Department, about midway between Chaumont and Neufchateau. Under the balmy June sun the surrounding green-cloaked hills or even the little field containing rows of barracks ready for occupation afforded a much more pleasing spectacle than the village itself, with its dirty streets through which cattle roamed at will. The rows of stone buildings seemed to represent the architectural skill and labor of the dark ages; at any rate, it represented nothing modern. Living rooms and cow stables were all one building. Wooden ladders led from the street below up to a second story hole-in-the-wall, and piles of manure made up the front yards. Manois had, undoubtedly, been a very quiet, sleepy village through the ages. Almost four years of war had drained it of all the vitalizing and pulsating influences which it might ever have possessed. The foundry just at the edge of the town was hardly in operation. The few girls, who were working there, begrimed with soot and dirt, looked like old bent women, as their frail, rounded shoulders bespoke manly efforts in pushing wheelbarrows and lifting heavy iron, that reels of wire might be turned out to meet the needs of France.

What the entry of the Battalion meant to the history of this little town and to the morale of the inhabitants can be realized only after one has had a more complete picture of the situation. Every available man was at the Front. Not even a French soldier in uniform could be seen on the streets. The crucial moment of the great war was at hand; Paris was now being bombarded daily, and one could faintly hear the distant roar of the large caliber guns as the fight waged around Chateau Thierry. Everything looked dark and foreboding. But now, the actual sight of American legions with their irrepressible and dominating spirit which fairly breathed an air of victory, could not but raise their hopes.

Colonel Reeves established Regimental Headquarters in Manois with the First Battalion. Changes in the town began to appear immediately. Streets were cleaned; small stores commenced to do business and town people took a renewed interest in life. Every evening the band gave concerts of popular American selections. On one occasion french troops from the sectors of Alsace and Lorraine were passing through the town. This meant that Americans were quietly and effectively relieving these experienced fighters at the Front. The troop train bound for Chateau Thierry and the North was stopped at the depot and the concert began. The appreciation of the troops manifested itself in hearty cheers. With greater determination they looked back as the train departed; each had his hat off and was standing at "Attention" for the "Marsellaise." These concerts brought the civilians and soldiers together and strengthened bonds of sympathy which made association increasingly pleasant as the days went by.

The schedule was doubly strenuous for the First Battalion. Scarcity of open ground resulted in the selection of a drill field upon a very high bluff. But this was part of the hardening process of intensive training. The march up to the drill field twice a day with the hot sun beating down on the tin hats and with full packs was more than a day's work in itself; many fell by the wayside during the first few days. But time unfolded joys as well as hardships. July brought the long awaited pay day. It was interesting to figure up centimes and francs at first but when it was learned that a franc was only nineteen cents and a centime was one one-hundredth of a franc the American doughboys generally paid in francs and called it square. Now they could buy fresh fruit and an occasional drop of vin rouge to supplement the "chow." And these purchases always included lessons in French. Mail from home brought more cheer into camp than anything else. Every man was on hand at mail call to shout "Yo" at the mention of his name. When the mail had all been distributed, the fortunate ones moved away to themselves and forgot they were in France. So the days of intensive training passed quickly by.

Scarcely two weeks had been spent in the Training Area until the First Battalion was called to represent the 89th Division in Chaumont. Chaumont was famous as the Headquarters of the American Expeditionary Forces. General Pershing with his entire staff was located there. A visit to this city was a coveted privilege, and the First Battalion of the 353rd Infantry was selected to parade before the Commander-in-Chief on July 14, the Independence Day of France.

The Regimental and Battalion Commanders spared no efforts to convince the reviewing authorities that the Regiment was ready for front line duties. The soldier who shortly before wore canvas leggins, and campaign hats with broad brim and a shoe-string chin strap was now transformed into an up-to-date soldier with spiral puttees and over-seas cap. The occasion itself could be depended upon to produce the military bearing. So they set out full of confidence.

The men had learned to march, and march well. It was eighteen dusty miles from Manois to Chaumont; the sun was stiflingly hot. Perhaps the thought of comfort was still unduly prominent in the minds of officers when they prescribed campaign hats and shirts for the march uniform. At any rate, a staff officer from Chaumont met the Battalion halfway and gave orders to wear blouses. "Under no condition would American soldiers appear in France without complete uniform!" In spite of this added handicap the men "carried on" and presented a fresh appearance in Chaumont on the evening of July 13. "Finest lot of soldiers I have seen yet," "Think of it, marched eighteen miles in the heat and dust with blouses and those packs on their backs and still look fresh." Such were the comments on all sides. These men of the 353rd Infantry had scored the first point — they had demonstrated that they could march.

Accommodations in Chaumont were far better than the men had been accustomed to in Manois. The clerks at Headquarters turned over their mess. Such "chow" and such service these men of the line had not known since leaving Camp Funston. And then, too, the excellent baths were an improvement over the little shallow stream in their own camp. Chaumont offered also a splendid opportunity to spend some of the francs for articles not available in Manois. Everybody needed razor blades and a change from Bull Durham tobacco. The Y.M.C.A. had a good canteen. Several real American girls were behind the counters. Such good company and an unusual amount of money (in francs) made business pleasant and interesting. Officers, too, were known to walk five squares in order to inquire about over-seas caps which the Y.M.C.A. did not have. The French shop keepers with their keen business sense had procured a good supply of over-seas caps but the sizes had been under-estimated, "Americaine head too beeg," repeated the little saleswoman in distress. In their hurry to meet the needs of customers, they had lost sight of size, the most important conditions of sale as well as service.

Incidentally, the men picked up quite a bit of information about what was expected of them on the following day. The Marines had been in town on this same mission just previously. Everybody was talking about the Marines. "They've set the pace, it's up to us to make a showing equally as good," was the mutual agreement. And with this in mind they turned in for the night.

The big day set in bright and hot, "Here's where I ditch my shirt," said one doughboy and the rest followed the example. They must continue to look fresh.

The formation had all been carefully planned. As the streets were narrow, companies marched in column of platoons of two squads each. The Battalion was well up to war strength of one thousand men, and the men were at their best. An Artillery Band led the way between the liens of people and passed the grand stand. At the command, "Eyes Right," each man "turned his head toward the right oblique and fixed his eyes" not as required in "Infantry Drill Regulation," "on the line of eyes of men in the same rank"; but as nearly as possible on the face of the Commander-in-Chief. They seemed to have been too busy watching the step and line and the position of their rifles to remember how he looked. When they returned all they could say was, "He's a soldier for you." The comment of the General at the reception for the offices later in the day indicated a very favorable impression. The First Battalion had scored again. Three weeks from the day of the parade the 89th Division was called to the Front.

While on the return journey the following day, word came from Andelot that coffee would be served at that place. Thus came into the life of the Regiment, Mother Fitzgerald and Miss Heermance. It later became impossible to tell whether they belong to the Regiment or whether the regiment belonged to them. During seven long weeks of heavy campaign, they stuck to their posts in the vicinity of Bouillonville, Beney and Gesnes to serve hot chocolate and coffee to the fighting men. They were Y.M.C.A. volunteers and served day in and day out without even removing a shoe until Colonel Reeves sent them back for rest. These were the good women who had sent the message from Andelot.

As the end of the journey neared, the men suffered from lack of water. It was hot and canteens had long since been emptied. An order limited the supply to one canteen for the trip, this being a part of the training for the trenches. Many became so desperate they broke ranks at a flowing fountain in a small town and disregarded the sign "Condemned Water."

These minor hardships led to what is known in the Army as "crabbing." It is often said that a good soldier is identified by the amount of "crabbing" he does. But in this war "crabbing" was dangerous; for enemy spies were ready to pick up information. The men of the First Battalion were surprised and humiliated by the following order:

General Order Number 9.

The following order is quoted for your information and compliance:

In conversing with numerous members of the newly arrived troops, Companies "A," "B," "C," and "D" of the 353rd Infantry, it was ascertained that they are only too willing to impart information. Full details were obtained of their trip across the Atlantic, their wretched stay of ten days in England, crossing the channel on a destroyer and an encounter en route. The name of their camp at Manois, the conditions there (bad water, fair food, not paid for several months, etc.) were discussed freely between themselves. It was further ascertained that they had not been directed to refrain discussing military matters.

Any violation of the above paragraph in the future will be followed by the most stringent disciplinary measures.

By Order of Lieutenant-Colonel Hawkins.

C.J. Masseck,
Captain, 353rd Infantry, Adjutant.

The unfortunate incident referred to in the order occurred in Chaumont. The men had made a good showing at the parade and they wished to make it clear that they had done so in spite of difficulties and their zeal in enhancing their triumph was charged against them as "crabbing." They had been misunderstood but this experience taught them a lesson which they never forgot.

The arrival at Manois was followed by resumption of the strenuous training schedule. Specialization began with increasing vigor. The men fairly tore up the dummies with their bayonets. Some were still afraid of grenades, but their fear only helped them to greater distance. No one was able to make high score with the Chauchat. The targets looked like they had been hit by fragments of a shell; yet the men insisted they had aimed and held the same for each shot. The French instructors contended that the effect of this dispersion was even more destructive to the morale of the enemy than direct hits, but the American soldiers were never satisfied with the result on the range and distrusted the Chauchat in campaigns. American officers from the Army Schools versed in the latest tactics and French officers direct from the Front were added as Regimental Instructors. More attention was now paid to extended formations than had been in the past but no formation was standard or final. Each new instructor and each succeeding pamphlet brought new combinations. All that they needed was information, and the formation took care of itself. While this instruction was indefinite and discouraging at the time it fitted well into the requirements of future campaigns.

The final touches of training were added in the trench system at Dome Fé. It was a preliminary movement to the Front. Each man carried his own equipment. The kitchens followed and the journey of nine miles was begun in final departure form. Each Battalion took its place in the outpost line in support and reserve. Reliefs were made even more conscientiously than they would ever be again at the Front. Actual demonstration of raid and patrol helped to clear up the theoretical instruction that had been received on the high bluff at Manois. When the First Battalion returned, the men were anxious to get to the front.

TELL OF 89TH'S FIGHTING
After First Test Middle West Men Were Made Shock Troops.
A Wounded Kansas Citian Describes Taking Mont Sec —
How One Yank Captured 600 Germans at St. Mihiel.

NEW YORK, Jan. 4. — The 89th Division has gone into Germany, its men from Missouri, Kansas, Colorado, Nebraska and South Dakota, part of the Army of Occupation, but the wounded who fell at the Argonne and St. Mihiel are returning. Lying in hospital beds or hobbling about the huge airy wards of Debarkation Hospital No. 3 here today, many of the heroes from the Middle West told of the conspicuous record made by the crack division Gen. Leonard Wood trained at Camp Funston.

The division first landed in England, remaining at Winchester for about a week, when they sailed from Southampton for Havre. After some time in training sectors they went into the line, first at Woevre, a quiet position in which they saw no real action.

"It was in our first action on the Troul sector," J.W. McClintock of Kansas City said, as he rested a "game" leg on the side of his bed, "that the 89th made such a showing it was designated as shock troopers and kept between the famous 1st and 2d divisions. We fought all of our most important engagements in that position."

TELLS OF TAKING MONT SEC.

McClintock told of the advance of September 12 in which the 89th and the 1st stormed opposite sides of the famous Hill 380, on which both French and British had suffered terrible losses. The hill, also known as Mont Sec, had been fortified by the Germans for four years and was considered almost impregnable. The 1st Division lay to the left, taking that side of the hill, while the 89th attacked the right. Starting at daybreak, McClintock's regiment, the 356th, passed through a ruined French village and took the wood at the foot of the hill, aided by tanks and following a most intensive 5-hour barrage. The hill itself was taken by 9 o'clock with comparatively few casualties. In the advance, McClintock says, the 89th had a 12-mile objective to make in four days. It required just forty-two hours to gain it, including taking the hill. It was on that advance that Major Bland was killed, McClintock being but a few yards away at the time.

Andrew O. Matson of Clay Center, KS, told of the reputation made by the 353d Regiment, which saw heavy action at St. Mihiel, the Toul and Argonne sectors.

"First Sergeant Adams of the 353d won the Distinguished Service Cross for capturing six hundred Germans," he said, and that was but one of many decorations awarded the men of the 89th As he waited the approach of the surgeon with fresh dressings, Matson described Sergeant Adams' unusual feat.

"I was in the St. Michiel action," Matson said. "The Fritzies were going backward so fast we sometimes had hard work keeping up with them. At once place Sergeant Adams noticed a bunch of them up ahead making for what appeared to be a group of dugouts. All he had was his revolver, but he fired at them and they ran down the dugout entrances. He covered the doorways with his gun and called for them to come out, which they did. By getting all of the Huns who surrendered from the dugouts and rounding up a few outside he got almost six hundred altogether and marched them back by himself. For this one-man surrounding of the Germans he received the D.S.C."

FOUGHT IN MUD AND RAIN.

Leander Richardson was with Company B of the 356th Regiment until October 22, when he was wounded in the Argonne Forest.

"Our company got ahead of the line in the Argonne," he said, "and we got so scattered in the underbrush there was only a platoon and a half left together under the command of Lieutenant Schwin, when we dug in for the night. The going was awful, and in addition to a driving rain the mud underfoot was slippery and deep. The trees had been fairly shot to pieces by shell fire, but the brush was so thick we couldn't see a man twenty-five yards away, and it was full of Hun machine guns. That was the worst fighting we had, but the men from the Middle West stood up wonderfully and earned many commendations." Richardson is from Marysville, Mo.

More than a hundred of the wounded from the 89th are at Debarkation Hospital No. 3 here or have been sent on to other hospitals for final recuperation.

FOCH FOR RHINE BARRIER

"There Must We Guard Our Victory," Says the Marshal.

"Let Us Remain United as We Were in Battle," He Tells Correspondents — Gives High Praise for the U.S. Fighters.

(By the Associated Press.)

TREVES, Jan. 15 (delayed). — It is the conviction of Marshal Foch that the Rhine must be made the barrier between Germany and France. He expressed this clearly today when he received American newspaper correspondents. The marshal is here in connection with the meeting concerning the extension of the armistice.

Marshal Foch pointed out the difficulties that had been overcome and said that peace must be commensurate with the price of victory. Germany now is beaten, he added, but with her resources, especially in men, recuperation in a comparatively short time is quite possible. It was now the duty of the Allies to prevent further aggressions.

Marshal Foch praised the work of the American troops, and said that General Pershing had asked that the American forces be concentrated for an attack on one sector. The Allied generalissimo admitted that the Argonne-Meuse front, where the American began their offense on September 26 was a "sector hard to tackle." The marshal said he had told General Pershing:

"Your men have the devil's own punch. They will get away with all that. Go to it."

The American attack succeeded, the marshal continued, "and here we are on the Rhine."

MAKE THE RHINE THE BARRIER.

"It is on the Rhine that we must hold the Germans. It is by using the Rhine that we must make it impossible for them to recommence the coup of 1914. The Rhine is the common barrier of all the Allies, precisely of all those who united to save civilization. The Rhine is the guarantee of peace for all the nations who have shed their blood in the cause of liberty. Then let us watch on the Rhine.

"We have no idea of attacking Germany or of recommencing the war. Democracies such as ours never attack. They ask but to live in peace and to grow in peace, but who can say that Germany — where democratic ideas are so recent and perhaps very superficial — will not quickly recover from its defeat?

"England has the channel to cross. America is far away. France must always be in a position to safeguard the general interests of mankind. These interests are at stake on the Rhine. It is there that we must prepare to guard against the painful surprises of the future.

ARMISTICE NOT TOO SOON.

The armistice was not concluded too soon and the Allies got all they asked for from Germany without continuing the fighting. The Allies, the marshal said, were prepared for another offensive stroke which would have forced the Germans to give up. This was to have been made in Lorraine on November 14 with six American and twenty French divisions.

"This is, for me," Marshal Foch began, "a happy opportunity to tell you all the good things I think of the American army and of the part it played on our side. Your soldiers were superb. They came to us young, enthusiastic and carried forward by a vigorous idealism and they marched to battle with admirable gallantry.

"Yes, they were superb. There is no other word. When they appeared our armies were, as you know, fatigued by three years of relentless struggle and the mantle of war lay heavily upon them. We were magnificently comforted by the virility of your Americans.

THE AMERICANS BROUGHT HOPE.

The youth of the United States brought a renewal of the hope that hastened victory. Not only was this moral fact of the highest importance, but you also brought enormous material aid and the wealth which you placed at our disposal contributed to the final success. Nobody among us will ever forget what America did.

"And you know what happened on the field of battle since the month of July — first on the Marne, then in the region of Verdun. General Pershing wished as far as possible to have his army concentrated in an American sector. The Argonne and the heights of the Meuse were a sector hard to tackle. There were considerable obstacles there.

"The German high command was not ignorant of the fact that it faced a colossal disaster. When it surrendered everything was prepared for an offensive in which it would infallibly have succumbed. On the 14th we were to attack in Lorraine with twenty French divisions and six American divisions. This attack would have been supported by other movements in Flanders and in the center.

"The Germans were lost. They capitulated. There is the whole story.

A PEACE TO MATCH VICTORY.

"And now we must make a peace which will correspond with the magnitude of our victory. We must have a peace as absolute as was our success and which will guard us against all future aggressions.

"France has a right to effective measures of protection after the formidable efforts she put forth to save civilization. The natural frontier which will protect civilization is the Rhine.

"The armistice is signed but peace is not yet concluded. So long as the status of Europe has not been settled, let us watch; let us watch together so that we lose not the fruits of our common victory. Let us remain united as we were in battle."

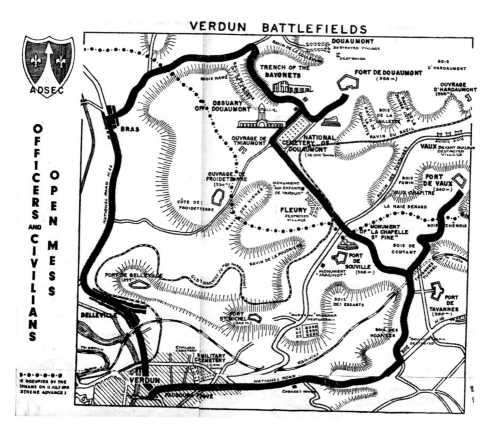

125

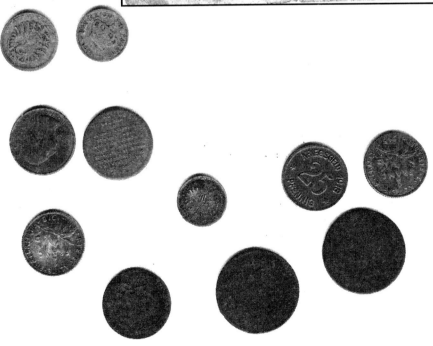

HOLD THE 35TH AND 89TH
The Home Divisions Not Scheduled for Early Return
None of the Kansas City or Other Missouri and Kansas Units Has Been Placed on Priority List for Early Transport.

(From the Star's Correspondent.)

WASHINGTON, Jan. 21. — Neither the 35th Division nor the 89th, the two combat units made up almost exclusively of Kansas and Missouri soldiers, are scheduled for early return home from France. The War Department has no word whatever on when they may be expected to return. The priority lists for sailings are made up on the other side by General Pershing's staff. The units that will start home in the next three or four weeks are on the priority list. Daily new additions are made to the lists. The fact that the famous 35th is not in the Army of Occupation points to the possibility of it getting home before the 89th.

THE 35TH AT COMMERCY.

The 35th is now stationed at Commercy, France. This is about twenty-five miles south and a little east of Verdun. It is near the old battle line, which, of course, is now far from the frontier. Around Commercy were thousands of American troops before the armistice, it being one of the large concentration centers. Whether the division will be stationed there until ordered broken up and sent home, or whether it will wait there until relieving some other unit in the Army of Occupation, there is no information here.

The Eighty-Ninth Division, the fighting unit Gen. Leonard Wood trained out at Funston, occupies one of the largest areas of the army of occupation. It is not on the Rhine, as many supposed, but back nearer France patrolling the largest individual area of Germany of any single American division. Roughly, the German territory the Kansans and Missourians patrol runs from a little south of Saarburg to a few miles north of Prumm. The division headquarters now are at Killburg, near the northern part of the area they patrol. They have almost a square chunk of Germany to keep in order.

THE 89TH PATROLS TREVES.

The most famous city in the area patrolled by the 89th is the old German cathedral city of Treves. A few weeks ago there was an advance detachment of the grand headquarters at Treves and headquarters troops, not the Kansas-Missouri division, patrolled the city itself, but it is probable the division now patrols the city.

Thus far there has been no sign of the Rainbow Division, the famous 42nd, being ordered home. It occupies the northernmost part of the area held by the Americans. The Kansas ammunition train and the Kansas City signal corps are in this division. Headquarters are at Ahrweiler. Questions as to when this division would get home met the reply, "not on the priority list yet." The 129th field artillery, another Kansas and Missouri unit, is in France, a little town of Moscow being given in the official dispatches as the headquarters. Moscow is not shown on the military maps. It is not on the priority list either. Base hospital unit 28, another Kansas City unit, is still at Limoges. Several other hospitals have got sailing orders, but no word has reached here of priority being given the Kansas City unit. The 92d Division, a negro division that trained at Funston and includes many Kansas and Missouri negro soldiers, is now at Murbach, France, down in the Vosges, close to the Swiss border. It also is not on the priority list as yet.

CAN'T PARADE HEROES HERE
Thirty-Fifth and 89th Will Not Be Intact When Returned.
Suitable Demonstrations Can Be Arranged for Individual Units on Way to Funston, General March Says

WASHINGTON, Feb. 8. — There will be no opportunity for the full 35th or 89th divisions to parade in Kansas City upon their return home. That was made plain by General March today in his weekly press statements. Individual regiments and units of those divisions will be sent to Funston for discharge intact, however, and suitable demonstrations can be made for them.

General March pointed out that while the divisions had left this country largely from certain localities, not even the National Guard divisions were purely local units now. There had been large replacements, and these replacements had come from everywhere in the country, so the entire complexion of many divisions had changed. The 35th Division made up of Missouri-Kansas National Guard, for example, has had ten thousand replacements from everywhere in the country. These replacements will be sent to the camps nearest their homes for discharge.

It is physically impossible to move any entire division at a time, General March pointed out. As a result, when the division starts coming home the troops will be arriving over a considerable period. The units will be broken up to the extent of sending the men to the camps nearest their homes for discharge.

END THEIR ARMY SERVICE
A Coach Loaded with Men Discharged at Camp Funston.

In a Letter to Each Man Maj. Gen. Leonard Wood Assures Men They Have Done a Soldier's Duty

WITH DISCHARGED SOLDIERS EN ROUTE FROM CAMP FUNSTON TO KANSAS CITY, Nov. 23. — We have with us tonight a railroad coach packed with howling and screeching, singing and yelling humanity. Riotous joy prevails. Morale is 200 per cent.

Clothed in regulation army uniform, these men have every appearance of being soldiers. An earful of their continuous hubbub corrects the erroneous idea.

Every man has a "scrap of paper" more precious to him than fine raiment or much gold. For the most part these papers are tucked away safely in an inside pocket. Some are being read and reread and flourished in the faces of other uniformed men.

"As a testimonial of honest and faithful service, hereby honorably discharged from the military service of the United States," one of the men reads from his paper.

"You know what that means to me?" he asks, and without waiting for an answer, rattles on.

"It means a wedding bell, a pair of pants loose at the bottom, a derby hat, a whole lot of homegrown eats and maybe a drink of something stronger than Bevo."

Having thoughts of his own, the unwilling audience tries to drive the speaker away, and fails.

"There's going to be an awful party in my home town," the excited orator continues, "when I get home. It's going to be a party for all the girls, with me the sole and only host. I can stay up late and parade around in peace without having to salute half the people I meet."

In broke a voice louder than all the rest.

"Boy, you ain't said a thing," the voice of the noisy one said. "What I'm going to do with this paper of mine is to paste it on the head of my bed and put up a big sign, 'Buglers Beware.' "

Another one expressed what his discharge meant to him.

"This paper is the death sentence of a certain flat-footed shoe clerk in my home town. He says he can't live without Madge, and Madge writes me she's been going with him just for fun. I'm going to stick closer to her now than I ever did to the mess hall in this man's army."

One fellow with a grouch hid away under his temporary happiness spoke up:

"Guys, that paper means it's an open season on lieuts and top-kickers. They been powerful fine and decent the last two weeks, because they know an open season was coming, but I ain't forgot how they treated me."

"We better heave our big times before those lucky devils get back from France," a pessimist suggested. "We'll get a little honor until they show up with gold stripes on their sleeves. Then we won't count much, and everybody will blame us because we never got into real fighting."

A LETTER TO EACH MAN.

Out came another official looking document, and excerpts were read and discussed. It was a personal farewell letter to every man discharged, written by Maj. Gen. Leonard Wood, camp commander.

General Wood had felt a personal interest in every man who entered his camp and took that means of expressing his appreciation of their spirit of willingness to serve.

Such an expression from "the chief," as most of the men reverently speak of him, means much to the enlisted man.

Similar letters will be given to each man as he is discharged.

Discharges will continue for many days under orders to reduce the depot brigade and development battalions. Approximately forty-five hundred men are to be mustered out under present orders. Other orders may be received at Camp Funston, but no further word had been received up until tonight.

"LEADING LADY" OF A.E.F.

Carl Schroeder of St. Louis Has Big Part in Yank Play.

"A Buck on Leave" Is a Real Soldier's Musical Comedy with Clever Effects and Pretty "Actresses."

H.H. Niemeyer in the St. Louis Post-Dispatch.

TOURS, FRANCE. — Every schoolboy and girl in the States can tell who the leading man of the American Army in France is without question. Even the school children in this country swear by General Pershing, but here in Tours, the center of the vast S.O.S. of the United States, there burst upon an unsuspecting public the leading lady of the American Army.

This is none other than Carl Schroeder of St. Louis, who, made up as a remarkably pretty girl, takes the leading role in the biggest and best show which the boys of the army have put on for their own entertainment and which is now touring the army camps of France.

There are eight "girls" in "A Buck on Leave," which is a vivid musical comedy splendidly played and splendidly staged by more than one hundred soldiers. In addition there is one real girl, Miss Orlo Lea Mayes, a little Y.M.C.A. canteen worker from Denver, but Miss Mayes is content to play a minor part and steps aside gracefully to make room for her eight "sisters," whom she assists in making up and who look very pretty indeed in their latest French costumes, made in Paris by the Y.M.C.A. under the direction of a famous French costumer.

SCHROEDER "OFF" AND "ON."

Schroeder is by no means a "lady" off the stage. For months he has been loading and unloading trucks in the S.O.S. and working in the great machine shop of the army at Verneuil. During rehearsals and when not on the stage he smokes big black cigars and chews tobacco, but when he is acting well, Julian Eltinge in his palmiest days had nothing on him.

"A Buck on Leave" is a real army show.

It was written by Sergt. Pat Barnes of Sharon, Pa., who plays the part of A. Buck; the music was composed by Lieut. Gordon Laughead of Toledo, who conducts the orchestra. Augustus Brunelle was responsible for the lyrics. The musical comedy is presented under the direction of Col. Harry A. Hageman of the Motor Transport Reconstruction Park, and the players in the big company, the orchestra, the scene painters, the carpenters and the electricians are all part of the personnel of the same organization.

EFFECT ON SOLDIERS.

The show is a remarkable one in many ways, and despite the fact that most of the jokes and most of the fun are poked at the officers of the army, from General Pershing down, it has the unqualified support of the army officials, for shortly after it was first produced it was discovered that the effect it had on its audience was good. The army has a way of checking up on the morals of the enlisted men, and in one week's run of the show the soldiers who came under observation of the army physicians dropped from several hundred a night to fourteen. That is one reason above all others why this show and similar shows are being encouraged, and why the army is glad to transport the entire company from town to town at no small expense to play in the big theaters which are furnished by the Y.M.C.A. Here in Tours, in one week, "A Buck on Leave" played before more than fifteen thousand officers and men and turned 'em away at every performance.

Being written by soldiers, the musical comedy is just what the soldiers want. To begin with, before the curtain goes up, an officious looking M.P. strolls down the aisle of the theater and orders a private out of the first row. "Don't you know," he asks, "that the front row is reserved for officers?"

The private gives up his seat, but as he goes out he says, "Is that so? Well, I never heard them telling us that up in the battle lines."

"PERSHING" AND "HARBORD"

General Pershing is portrayed true to life by Percy Franzman, a big private who is made up to closely resemble the American commander. Harley Young, another private, is General Harbord, the commander of the S.O.S., and in the play they meet A. Buck in a hotel in Aix-les-Bains and tell him he may go as far as he likes while on furlough and then they help him have a good time.

There is plenty of good music in the show and plenty of good scenery and many startling electrical effects. It is not possible for the big company to carry around its own scenery from town to town, but just as soon as the organization is booked in a city the staff of carpenters and painters and electricians go ahead and build a new set.

The show had its beginning many months ago when Lieutenant Laughead organized a band among the motor transport repair park boys with just a few instruments and men. Now there are seventy-five men in the band and orchestra, and there is a saxophone band of twelve and a trained chorus of fifty voices, around which the musical comedy has been constructed.

PERSHING'S TRIBUTE

"Men of the Line" the Heroes of America's Part in the World War, Says the General

"THEIR DEEDS IMMORTAL"

A Crisis Faced the Allies When Yanks Went In, and They Met Every Task Unflinchingly, He says.

The Commander's Own Story of the Nation's Place in the Conflict Given to Secretary Baker.

TURNED TIDE BEFORE PARIS

The General Tells of Lack of Equipment and Delays Incident to Our Unpreparedness.

(By the Associated Press)

WASHINGTON, Dec. 4. — Gen. John J. Pershing's account of his stewardship as commander of the American Expeditionary Forces was given to the public today by Secretary Baker. It is in the form of a preliminary report to the secretary, covering operations up to November 20, after the German collapse. It closed with these words from the leaders of the great army in France, expressing his feeling for those who served under him.

"I pay the supreme tribute to our officers and soldiers of the line. When I think of their heroism, their patience under hardships, their unflinching spirit of offensive action, I am filled with emotion which I am unable to express. Their deeds are immortal, and they have earned the eternal gratitude of our country."

The report begins with General Pershing's departure for France to pave the way for the army that was to smash German resistance on the Meuse and give vital aid to the Allies in forcing Germany to its knees nineteen months later. Its striking feature is the section devoted to "combat operations," where it told the story of fighting by the man who directed it.

General Pershing views the encounters before March 21 of this year in which American troops participated as a part of their training, and dismisses them briefly. On that date, however, the great German offensive was launched and a crucial situation quickly developed in the Allied lines which called for prompt use of the four American divisions that were at that time "equal to any demands of battle action."

The first crisis of the German drive had been reached in Picardy.

"The crisis which this offensive developed was such," General Pershing says, "that our occupation of an American sector must be postponed. On March 28 I placed at the disposal of Marshal Foch, who had been agreed upon as commander-in-chief of the Allied armies, all of our forces to be used as he might decide. At his request the First Division was transferred from the Toul sector to a position in reserve at Chaumont en Vexin. As German superiority in numbers required prompt action, an agreement was reached at the Abbeville conference of the Allied premiers and commanders and myself on May 2, by which British shipping was to transport ten American divisions to the British army area, where they were to be trained and equipped, and additional British shipping was to be provided for as many divisions as possible for use elsewhere.

"On April 26 the 1st Division had gone into the line in the Montdidier salient on the Picardy battle front. Tactics had been suddenly revolutionized to those of open warfare, and our men, confident of the results of their training, were eager for the test. On the morning of May 28 this division attacked the commanding German position in its front, taking with splendid dash the town of Cantiguy and all other objectives, which were organized and held steadfastly against vicious counter attacks and galling artillery fire. Although local, this brilliant action had an electrical effect, as it demonstrated our fighting qualities under extreme battle conditions, and also that the enemy's troops were not altogether invincible."

There followed immediately the German thrust across the Aisne toward Paris.

"The Allies," General Pershing says, "faced a crisis equally as grave as that of the Picardy offensive in March. Again every available man was placed at Marshal Foch's disposal, and the 3d Division, which had just come from its preliminary training in the trenches, was hurried to the Marne. Its motorized machine gun battalion preceded the other units and successfully held the bridgehead at the Marne opposite Chateau Thierry. The 2d Division, in reserve near Montdidier, was sent by motor trucks and other available transport to check the progress of the enemy toward Paris. The division attacked and retook the town and railroad station at Bouresches and sturdily held its ground against the enemy's best guard divisions.

"In the Battle of Belleau Wood, which followed, our men proved their superiority and gained a strong tactical position, with far greater loss to the enemy than to ourselves. On July 1, before the 2d was relieved, it captured the village of Vaux with most splendid precision.

"Meanwhile, our second corps, under Maj. Gen. George W. Read, had been organized for the command of our divisions with the British, which were held back in training areas or assigned to second line defenses. Five of the ten divisions were withdrawn from the British area in June, three to relieve divisions in Lorraine and the Vosges and two to the Paris area to join the group of American divisions which stood between the city and any further advance of the enemy in that direction.

By that time the great tide of American troop movements to France was in full swing and the older divisions could be used freely. The 42d, in line east of Reims, faced the German assault of July 15 and "held their ground unflinchingly;" on the right

flank four companies of the 28th Division faced "advancing waves of German infantry" and the 3d Division held the Marne line opposite Chateau Thierry against powerful artillery and infantry attack.

"A single regiment of the 3d wrote one of the most brilliant pages in our military annals on this occasion," General Pershing says. "It prevented the crossing at certain points on its front while, on either flank, the Germans who had gained a footing pressed forward. Our men, firing in three directions, met the German attacks with counter attacks at critical points and succeeded in throwing two German divisions into complete confusion, capturing six hundred prisoners."

Thus was the stage set for the counter offensive which, beginning with the smashing of the enemy's Marne salient, brought overwhelming victory to the Allies and the United States in the eventful months that have followed. The intimation is strong that General Pershing's advice helped Marshal Foch to reach his decision to strike. General Pershing continues:

"The great force of the German Chateau Thierry offensive established the deep Marne salient, but the enemy was taking chances, and the vulnerability of this pocket to attack might be turned to his disadvantage. Seizing this opportunity to support my conviction, every division with any sort of training was made available for use in a counter offensive. The place of honor in the thrust toward Soissons on July 18 was given to our 1st and 2d divisions in company with chosen French divisions.

"Without the usual brief warning of a preliminary bombardment, the massed French and American artillery, firing by the map, laid down its rolling barrage at dawn while the infantry began its charge. The tactical handling of our troops under these trying conditions was excellent throughout the action. The enemy brought up large numbers of reserves and made a stubborn defense both with machine guns and artillery, but through five days' fighting the 1st Division continued to advance until it had gained the heights above Soissons and captured the village of Berzy-le-sec. The 2d Division took Beau Repaire Farm and Vierzy in a very rapid advance and reached a position in front of Tigny at the end of its second day. These two divisions captured seven thousand prisoners and over one hundred pieces of artillery."

The report describes in some detail the work of completing the reduction of the salient, mentioning the operations of the 26th, 3d, 4th, 42d, 32d and 28th divisions. With the situation on the Marne front thus relieved, General Pershing writes, he could turn to the organization of the 1st American Army and the reduction of the St. Mihiel salient, long planned as the initial purely American enterprise. A troop concentration, aided by generous contributions of artillery and air units by the French, began, involving the movement, mostly at night, of six hundred thousand men. A sector reaching from Port sur Seille, east of the Moselle, westward through St. Mihiel to Verdun and later enlarged to carry it to the edge of the forest of Argonne, was taken over, the 2d Colonial French holding the tip of the salient opposite St. Mihiel, and the French 17th Corps, on the heights above Verdun, being transferred to general Pershing's command.

The combined French, British and American air forced mobilized for the battle, the report says, was the largest aviation assembly ever engaged on the western front up to that time in a single operation.

Of the reduction of the St. Mihiel salient, General Pershing says:

"After four hours artillery preparation the seven American divisions in the front line advanced at 5 a.m., on September 12, assisted by a limited number of tanks manned partly by the French. These divisions, accompanied by groups of wire cutters and others armed with bangalore torpedoes, went through the successive bands of barbed wire that protected the enemy's front line and support trenches, in irresistible waves on schedule time, breaking down all defense of an enemy demoralized by the great volume of our artillery

fire and our sudden approach out of the fog.

"Our first corps advanced to Thiaucourt, while our fourth corps curved back to the southwest through Nonsard. The Second Colonial French corps made the slight advance required of it on very difficult ground, and the fifth corps took its three ridges and repulsed a counter attack. A rapid march brought reserve regiments of a division of the fifth corps into Vigneulles in the early morning, where it linked up with patrols of our fourth corps, closing the salient and forming a new line west of Thiaucourt to Vigneulles, and beyond Fresnes-en-Woevre.

"At the cost of only seven thousand casualties, mostly light, we had taken sixteen thousand prisoners and 443 guns, a great quantity of material, released the inhabitants of many villages from enemy domination, and established our lines in a position to threaten Metz.

"This signal success of the American First Army in its first offensive was of prime importance. The Allies found they had a formidable army to aid them, and the enemy learned finally that he had one to reckon with."

The report shows for the first time, officially, that with this brilliantly executed coup, General Pershing's men had cleared the way for the great effort of the Allies and American forces to win a conclusive victory. The American army moved at once toward its crowning achievement, the Battle of the Meuse.

The general tells a dramatic story of this mighty battle in three distinct phases, beginning on the night of September 27, when Americans quickly took the places of the French on the thinly held line of this long quiet sector. The attacked opened on September 26, and the Americans drove through entanglements, across No Man's Land to take all the enemy's first line positions.

Closing the chapter, General Pershing says:

"On November 6 a division of the 1st Corps reached a point on the Meuse opposite Sedan, twenty-five miles from our line of departure. The strategical goal which was our highest hope was gained. We had cut the enemy's main line of communications, and nothing but surrender or an armistice could save his army from complete disaster.

"In all forty enemy divisions had been used against us in the Meuse-Argonne battle. Between September 26 and November 6 we took 26,059 prisoners and 468 guns on this front. Our divisions engaged were the 1st, 2d, 3d, 4th, 5th, 26th, 28th, 29th, 32d, 33d, 335th, 37th, 42d, 77th, 78th, 79th, 80th, 82d, 89th, 90th and 91st. Many of our divisions remained in line for a length of time that required nerves of steel, while others were sent in again after only a few days of rest. The 1st, 5th, 26th, 42d, 77th, 80th, 89th and 90th were in the line twice. Although some of the divisions were fighting their first battle, they soon became equal to the best."

The commander-in-chief does not lose sight of the divisions operating with French or British armies during this time. He tells of the work of the 2d Corps, comprising the 27th and 30th Divisions in the British assault on the Hindenburg line where the St. Quentin canal passes through a tunnel; of how the 2d and 36th Divisions got their chance in October by being assigned to aid the French in the drive from Reims and of the splendid fighting of the 37th and 91st Divisions sent to join the French Army in Belgium.

Of the total strength of the Expeditionary Force, General Pershing reports:

"There are in Europe altogether, including a regiment and some sanitary units with the Italian army and the organizations at Murmansk, also including those en route from the States, approximately 2,053,347 men, less our losses. Of this total there are in France 1,338,169 combatant troops. Forty divisions have arrived, of which the infantry personnel of ten have been used as replacements, leaving thirty divisions now in France organized into three armies of three corps each."

Of their equipment he says:

"Our entry into the war found us with few of the auxiliaries necessary for its conduct in the modern sense. Among our most important deficiencies in material were artillery, aviation and tanks. In order to meet our requirements as rapidly as possible, we accepted the offer of the French government to provide us with the necessary artillery equipment of seventy-fives, one fifty-five millimeter howitzers and one fifty-five G.P.F. guns from their own factories for thirty divisions. The wisdom of this course is fully demonstrated by the fact that, although we soon began the manufacture of these classes of guns at home, there were no guns of the caliber mentioned manufactured in America on our front at the date the armistice was signed. The only guns of these types produced at home thus far received in France are 109 Seventy-five millimeter guns.

"In aviation we were in the same situation, and here again the French government came to our aid until our own aviation program should be under way. We obtained from the French the necessary planes for training our personnel, and they have provided us with a total of 2,676 pursuit, observation and bombing planes. The first airplanes received from home arrived in May, and altogether we have received 1,379. The first American squadron completely equipped by American production, including airplanes, crossed the German lines on August 7, 1918. As to tanks, we were also compelled to rely upon the French. Here, however, we were less fortunate, for the reason that the French production could barely meet the requirements of their own armies.

"It should be fully realized that the French government has always taken a most liberal attitude and has been most anxious to give us every possible assistance in meeting our deficiencies in these as well as in other respects. Our dependence upon France for artillery, aviation and tanks was, of course, due to the fact that our industries had not been exclusively devoted to military production. All credit is due our own manufacturers for their efforts to meet our requirements, as at the time the armistice was signed we were able to look forward to the early supply of practically all our necessities for our own factories."

PERSHING A MORAL FORCE

Through His Leadership Men Will Come Back Clean.

Dr. George H. Combs Praises American General in First Sermon Since His Return from Trip to France — Resumes His Pastorate.

"If the American soldiers do not come back clean, it will not be General Pershing's fault," Dr. George H. Combs, pastor of the Independence Boulevard Christian Church, said in an address there last night. At the services last night Doctor Combs resumed the pastorate of the church after a year's leave of absence. He has just returned from four months spent in welfare work under the auspices of the Red Triangle with the American soldiers in France.

The church was crowded with an audience anxious to hear of his experiences overseas and to welcome him back.

Continuing, Doctor Combs said in part:

"The Nation is under an eternal debt of gratitude to General Pershing for his splendid efforts on behalf of the welfare of our army. He has done everything possible to make the path of rectitude the easy and proper one for them. His utterances on all moral subjects have been worthy of the highest pulpits of the land. The English soldier had his rum, the French *poilu* his wine, the Yankee plain water — and the memory of his mother."

Doctor Combs drew a graphic picture of the conditions in France at the present time.

IS A NEW FRANCE.

Bismarck said that in the next war Germany would bleed France white. After more than four years of the most terrible warfare, I am happy to be able to say his prophecy has failed of fulfillment. France is not exhausted, tottering, forlorn, or disheartened. Despite all of her sufferings, the country has emerged with a new life and a new quickening of spirit. The port cities are actually on the boom, the factories are busy, agriculture has come into its own again. The American army revived France industrially even as it saved it by the might of its arms.

CLOSE TO AMERICA.

"France has suffered, but she will never forget her obligation to America. Nothing, I believe, could estrange the two countries. It is the man on the street, the simple peasant, the soldier who loves us most. Paris is still under the spell of the terrible days of last March, when the British armies were defeated as they had not been defeated in five hundred years. France knows that America came to the rescue and gave of her best and would have continued to give as long as it might be necessary.

In the streets the little children have learned enough English to sing in their quavering voices, 'Hail, Hail, the Gang's All Here.' They love us, the whole nation loves us."

G. H. Q.
AMERICAN EXPEDITIONARY FORCES,

GENERAL ORDERS}
No. 38-A. }

FRANCE, *February 28, 1919.*

MY FELLOW SOLDIERS:

Now that your service with the American Expeditionary Forces is about to terminate, I can not let you go without a personal word. At the call to arms, the patriotic young manhood of America eagerly responded and became the formidable army whose decisive victories testify to its efficiency and its valor. With the support of the nation firmly united to defend the cause of liberty, our army has executed the will of the people with resolute purpose. Our democracy has been tested, and the forces of autocracy have been defeated. To the glory of the citizen-soldier, our troops have faithfully fulfilled their trust, and in a succession of brilliant offensives have overcome the menace to our civilization.

As an individual, your part in the world war has been an important one in the sum total of our achievements. Whether keeping lonely vigil in the trenches, or gallantly storming the enemy's stronghold; whether enduring monotonous drudgery at the rear, or sustaining the fighting line at the front, each has bravely and efficiently played his part. By willing sacrifice of personal rights; by cheerful endurance of hardship and privation; by vigor, strength and indomitable will, made effective by thorough organization and cordial co-operation, you inspired the war-worn Allies with new life and turned the tide of threatened defeat into overwhelming victory.

With a consecrated devotion to duty and a will to conquer, you have loyally served your country. By your exemplary conduct a standard has been established and maintained never before attained by any army. With mind and body as clean and strong as the decisive blows you delivered against the foe, you are soon to return to the pursuits of peace. In leaving the scenes of your victories, may I ask that you carry home your high ideals and continue to live as you have served—an honor to the principles for which you have fought and to the fallen comrades you leave behind.

It is with pride in our success that I extend to you my sincere thanks for your splendid service to the army and to the nation.

Faithfully,

John J. Pershing

OFFICIAL:
  ROBERT C. DAVIS,
    Adjutant General.

Commander in Chief.

Copy furnished to **Gardner George W.**

Ward A Gardner

1st Lieut. 353rd Infantry

Commanding.

137

THE GLORY TO DOUGHBOYS
Infantryman the Big Factor of War, Says Lieut. G.B. Kellogg.
Returned Kansas City Officer, Who Remained with Men Two Days After Being Wounded, Praises 89th Division.

"It was the intelligent, ever resourceful, hard fighting American doughboys, who by their unquenchable enthusiasm and consistently victorious advanced, put the pep into the war and made the signing of the armistice possible. To them belongs the glory."

That was the tribute paid the American infantrymen by Lieut. G.B. Kellogg of the 354th United States Infantry, 89th Division, who returned to Kansas City yesterday, following six months' service in France. Lieutenant Kellogg, who before his enlistment was associated with his brother, Scott P. Kellogg, in the Kellogg Investment Company, was commissioned at the first officers' training camp at Fort Riley, Kas. He went over with the 89th Division last June, and saw active service until November 3. November 1 his temporary dugout was shattered by a high explosive shell, and Lieutenant Kellogg suffered a fractured collar bone. He remained with his company two days longer, when he was sent to the hospital. After more than a month there, he was invalided home, landed at Newport News a week ago.

"There is no question," Lieutenant Kellogg said, "that the American infantryman leads the world. In my judgment this war depended more upon the individual soldier than any other great contest of modern times. Despite all the recent inventions of warfare and war's tremendous complexity, in the final analysis men counted. After the plan of battle had been laid out, it was not a matter of tactics. Certain objectives were mapped out. All the advance information possible was secured. But much necessarily was not learned. The battle then passed from the staff officers into that of the men. Then it was that the resourcefulness, initiative and matchless daring of the infantrymen came into play. Artillery, airplanes and tanks, all the adjuncts of war, were necessary, but it was the doughboys who captured the objectives. I am happy report that the men of the 89th Division stood up with the very best of the American army."

Discussing the reduction of the St. Mihiel salient, Lieutenant Kellogg said that while the Germans had perhaps figured upon eventually leaving the salient, they left when they did because they could not stand the pressure of the American forces.

"They were not expecting or accustomed to ceaseless hammer blows that pinched in and cut off their advance lines before they were awake to the situation. They were given no chance to rest or repair their positions. Our soldiers were ever at their throats. When the salient was reduced, we found permanent dugouts and headquarters far better than we had been accustomed to. Our dead was buried near a German cemetery, and I have no doubt some Kansas City boys lie there today."

Lieutenant Kellogg said the equipment of the 89th Division was complete in every detail and that there was an abundance of all supplies. "We had more ammunition, bombs and hand grenades than we could shoot away," he said.

The fighting in and around Bantheville, in the closing days of the war, so far as the 89th was concerned, was characterized as even more severe, with heavier casualties, than at St. Mihiel.

"The artillery action was very severe," Lieutenant Kellogg continued, "and the men were subjected to a withering machine gun fire.

"Perhaps the most interesting phases of a battlefield are behind the front lines. It was marvelous to see the supports come up after an objective had been taken. It was almost uncanny in its regularity. First, the waves of the relieving force, then the light, later the heavy artillery, the supply wagons, ambulance, dressing stations, engineers, signal corps and finally brigade headquarters."

GEO. GARDNER WRITES FROM GERMANY.

Rommersheim, Germany
Dec. 28, 1918

Dear Sis and family:

Just now received a letter from you, also one from mother. So as I have nothing to do will write a few lines. Your letter was dated the 30th of November and mother's the 29th. Yes, I got the handkerchief that you and mother sent to me. I gave one of them to Sergt. Dozer and I have the other one yet and it is ready for the wash tub now. Yes, you tell 'em I am glad the war is over, but I wish they would send us back to the states. I don't like this country. This morning there was about four inches of snow on the ground and now it is all gone. Has been raining all day. In fact, it rains nearly all the time here in winter time but don't get very cold, I guess. Would like to get home in time to go rabbit hunting, but am quite sure I will not. A nice rabbit wouldn't go bad for supper. We were at Stenary, France, when the armistice was signed. We left there on the 24th of November for Germany. We were in Belgium on Thanksgiving (Chantemelle was the name of the town.) We came thru Belgium, Luxemburg and landed in Germany on Dec. 6th about 1:15 o'clock p.m. The Germans treat us fine, but I guess it's because they have to. Well, it's time for retreat so will finish this after supper. We have retreat at 3:30 o'clock. It is dark at 4 o'clock.

Retreat is over and isn't hardly time for supper yet, so will proceed to write a little more. We usually have supper at 4 o'clock on account of it getting dark so early, but the days will soon begin to get longer and then we won't have to eat so early.

Now a little about this country, buildings, etc. The country is rather rough and lots of trees of all kinds. A great many evergreens. Some of the nicest scenery that you ever saw, if it was only in the states, but it is in the wrong country to ever do us any good. The people thrash their grain with a flail. Once in a while they will have a machine that they call a threshing machine. It is a power, usually pulled by a horse or oxen. They work their milk cows, also dogs. It looks like children playing to see them driving dogs. The buildings are all made of stone. House and barn are in the same building. Sometimes they have a door out of the kitchen right into the barn. Pig pen, chicken house, barn and house all in the same building. That's going some, isn't it? Well, I must go to supper as it is five minutes till 4 o'clock. Will finish after supper if I think of anything to say.

Well, supper is over and I believe I feel worse now than I did before I ate. We had boiled beef, mashed potatoes, gravy and soup. I believe I told mother that I lost Randolph's address. I thought I had but I found it and wrote to him a few days ago. I haven't heard from him yet. Well, I expect you will be tired of reading when you get through with this so will close for this time. I wrote to mother a few days ago. Good night.

Your brother, Sergt. Geo. W. Gardner
Co. F 353rd Inf., A.E.F., P.O. 161

From the *Herald* files

Aug. 18, 1918

The German Offensive of 1918

The 1918 offensive of the German army, carefully planned at Berlin, was intended to overcome the Allies before American could brng any effective number of her troops. The successive German drives, which began March 21st, have now become history ... To meet these various drives, the Allies under GeneralFoch adopted the tactics of a slow and cautious retreat.

In the July drive, General Foch felt himself strong enough to inaugurate a policy of counter-attack. The German's crown prince threw his forced forward in a slant across the Marne. Successive French-American attacks imperiled the position of the German army and brought about its retreat ... The balance is again swinging toward the Allies. On the one side is a great army advancing, full of hope, with the certainty of a constant addition of fresh enthusiastic troops ... We look upon the present situation as the beginning of the end, and trust that this forward movement of the Allies will be halted only when it has swept through the last of German defenses.

Nov. 7, 1918

Germany Accepts

A phone message today noon says that a wire had just been received saying that Germany has accepted the Allies terms.

Nov. 14, 1918

Germany Surrenders Unconditionally

The strictly military terms of the armistice with Germany are embraced in eleven specifications which include the evacuation of all invaded territories, the withdrawal of the German troops from the left bank of the Rhine and the surrender of all supplies of war.

The military terms include the surrender of 5,000 guns, half field and half artillery; 30,000 machine guns, 3,000 flame throwers and 2,000 airplanes.

Nov. 14, 1918

Big Noise

On Monday afternoon and evening the city went wild over the news that the war was over. Delegations of people young and old paraded ther street, cheering and blowing horns and firing guns, making a regular bedlam. The Kaiser was dragged in effigy through the streets with a rope around his neck ...

And in the same issue ...

The War Is Ended

That people now living have been permitted to see one of the greatest carnivals of blood known in the history of the past 1,000 years is doubtless true. The coterie of politicians that surrounded the Kaiser are the ones who are resally to blame for the loss of 4 million of men in the prime of life is the truth ... That it will be impossible to adequately punish so inhumane a monster is true, but if he and his crowd are allowed to go to some neutral country and live the balance of their days in luxury and indolence will be a miscarriage of justice that ought not be allowed.

— E.M. Coldren, editor

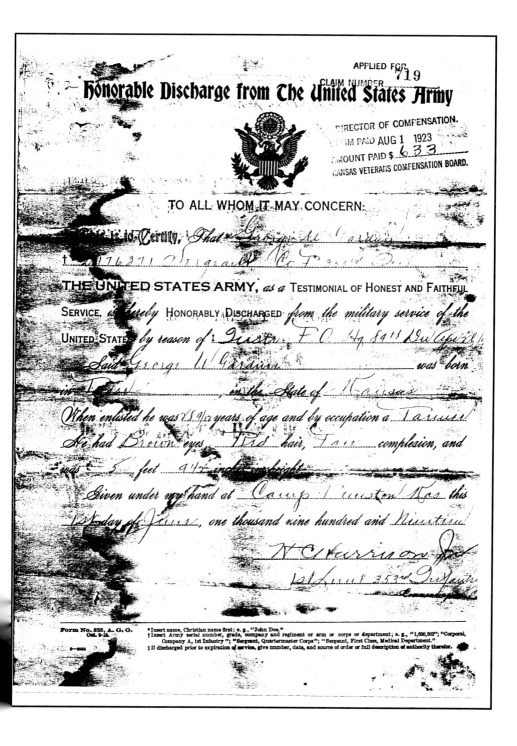

Honorable Discharge from The United States Army

TO ALL WHOM IT MAY CONCERN:

This is to Certify, That *George W Gardner*

† 2176371 Sergeant Co F 2nd In.

THE UNITED STATES ARMY, *as a* TESTIMONIAL OF HONEST AND FAITHFUL

SERVICE, *is hereby* HONORABLY DISCHARGED *from the military service of the*

UNITED STATES *by reason of* ‡ *Quartr. F C Hq 89th Div April 6*

Said George W Gardner *was born*

in Paola *, in the State of Kansas*

When enlisted he was 18 9/12 *years of age and by occupation a* Farmer

He had Brown *eyes,* Red *hair,* Fair *complexion, and*

was 5 *feet* 9 1/2 *inches in height.*

Given under my hand at Camp Funston Kas *this*

1st *day of* June *, one thousand nine hundred and* Nineteen

W C Harrison Jr
1st Lieut 353rd Infantry
Commanding

Form No. 525, A. G. O.
Oct. 9-18.

* Insert name, Christian name first; e. g., "John Doe."
† Insert Army serial number, grade, company and regiment or arm or corps or department; e. g., "1,620,302"; "Corporal, Company A, 1st Infantry"; "Sergeant, Quartermaster Corps"; "Sergeant, First Class, Medical Department."
‡ If discharged prior to expiration of service, give number, date, and source of order or full description of authority therefor.

WEARYIN' FOR YOU

Someone sends in, with evident approbation, the following poem from the Monitor, published at Grandview, Ind.:

I'M TIRED

I'm tired, oh, so tired, of the whole
    new deal,
Of the juggler's smile, the barker's
    spiel,
Of the mushy speech and the loud
    bassoon,
And tiredest of all of our leader's
    croon.

Tired of taxes on my ham and eggs,
Tired of "pay-offs" to political yeggs,
Tired of Jim Farley's stamp on my
    mail,
Tired of my shirt with its tax-
    shortened tail.

I'm tired of farmers goose-stepping to
    laws,
Of millions of itching job-holders'
    paws.
Of "fire-side talks" over
    commandeered "mikes,"
Of passing more laws to stimulate
    strikes.

I'm tired of the hourly increasing
    debt,
I'm tired of promises still to be met,
Of eating and sleeping by
    government plan,
Of calmly forgetting the "forgotten
    man."

I'm tired of every new brain trust
    thought,
Of the Ship of State — now a
    pleasure yacht,
I'm tied of steering the courts by
    stealth,
And terribly tired of sharing my
    wealth.

I'm tired of Eleanor on page one,
Of each royal in-law and favorite
    son,
I'm tired of Sistie and Buzzie Dall,
I'm simply, completely, fed up on it
    all.

RETURN AND DEMOBILIZATION

This was to be the final move of the 353rd Infantry. In the preceding changes of position there was some possibility of return; at any rate, another move would be sure to follow. But when the regiment left the area of occupation in Germany, demobilization was to follow and service ended not merely in the Army of Occupation but in the Army of the United States. So this more involved not merely a change of position but a return to civilian life.

Good Ship Leviathan.
This was the ship my father came home on.

Even a change of position means a busy time but never before had the officers and enlisted men of the 353rd Infantry experienced such a rush as during the final days in the Army of Occupation. The regiment must be ready on schedule time, and woe to the man who would look back once the movement was begun. Ready to move meant that the men were personally inspected, thoroughly equipped and properly recorded; that all surplus property had been turned in; that the billets had been set in order and the towns policed; that all accounts had been closed; that provision had been made for the trip. All these things must be done to the satisfaction of G.H.Q. inspectors. These gentlemen must approve the past and present and place their guarantee upon provisions for the future. Any slip-up might cause the division to lose out on the sailing date, so each man accepted full responsibility for his bunkie and all agree to see that the 353rd Infantry was ready to move on time.

Reports had come back of "show down" inspections at the dock. It was enough to endure the hardship of war and at this late date no one cared to take chances on a court martial, so souvenirs went with the surplus.

These matters concerned the men as individuals; there were requirements equally exacting for the organization as a whole. On April 23, Lieut. H.F. (Light) Browne issued the following memorandum to supply sergeants:

> "The Regimental Supply Company must turn in all surplus Q.M. property of this regiment in Bitburg at nine o'clock on April 26. In order to do this, surplus property now held in companies just be ready by noon April 26. This schedule has been set by the division and we must comply with it. Do not stop until you have turned in all your property, even though it is necessary to work all Thursday night.
>
> "Attention is called to a change in the list of property to be retained. Only one pair of shoes will be kept by each soldier instead of two pairs. Shoes turned in should be tied together."

The special precaution about tying shoes together is slightly indicative of the value set on time during these days. Animals must be turned in at Trier and Wengeroth on May 1st and 2nd. This increased the problem of collecting material and distributing rations but the Supply Company of the 353rd Infantry was on hand at the appointed hour.

With the surplus property out of the way, policing billets and towns became a simple matter. The men carefully rolled their packs so as to make sure of their possessions and carried them to the street. When they returned they had nothing to do but "make a cleanin' " and they did it with a vengeance. Another skirmish through the streets completed the police to the satisfaction of the inspectors.

It remained now to square accounts with the civilian population. Proclamations had been posted notifying them to turn in all claims for damage. Officers were required to pay for messes and kitchen. Final settlements were largely in the hands of the town majors. These town majors must have clearance receipts from the burgermeister within their area. All claims must be settled before leaving the posts. When the train pulled in every man, town majors and all, were waiting to go aboard.

The first trains were made up of forty cars (hommes-chevaux type), one coach for officers together with two of the former type, sleeping cars for officers, one kitchen car and two baggage cars. Each train carried approximately nine hundred men and fifty officers. The first train left on the evening of May 6th; the second followed early in the morning of May 7th, and the last train with Regimental Headquarters, Headquarters Company, Companies "A" and "B" and some artillery troops at 8:07 p.m. May 7th.

Left to right: Lt. Gen. Alphonse Jacques, France; Gen. Armando Diaz, Italy; Marshall Ferdinand Foch, France; Gen. John J. Pershing, U.S.A.; Adm. Sir Wm. Beatty, Great Britain.

Original print made and sold by the young professional photographer who slipped through the crowd and made the only photo of the dignitaries. The date was November 1, 1921.

STATE OF KANSAS
—

OFFICE OF SECRETARY OF STATE
E.A. Cornell, Chief
AUTOMOBILE REGISTRATION DEPARTMENT
TOPEKA

July 7th, 1922.

Geo. Gardner, Sheriff,
Oberlin, Kansas.

Dear Sir:

  I am just in receipt of your letter of July 6th relative to complaint made to your office regarding use of truck tag 17,965, with also a letter relative to the same matter from Judge Geiger.
  I am writing the Judge and enclose herewith a copy of letter which will also answer yours.
          Very truly yours,

        E.A. Cornell

EAC:RV

Dad went into law enforcement after the war.

146

DEPARTMENT OF COMMERCE
BUREAU OF THE CENSUS
WASHINGTON

July 10, 1922

Dear Sir:

At this writing no reply has been received to my request of June 25, 1922, for a statement of the number of persons in confinement on July 1, 1922, as compared with the number July 1, 1917, or careful estimate for 1917 if the actual number is not available.

It is extremely important that this information be supplied without delay, in order that the results of this preliminary count of the number of prisoners in the United States may be made public at the very earliest date possible. An immediate reply, if it has not already been sent, will be greatly appreciated.

Very respectfully,

W.M. Stewart
Director

Sheriff of Decatur County,
Oberlin, Kansas

SHERIFF CATCHES FORD COUNTY WIFE

Our Own George Gardner United in Marriage at Dodge City Last Week.

Friends of sheriff-elect, George W. Gardner, were surprised the first of the week to learn of his marriage on December 8th, to Miss Margaret Slocum, of Dodge City, Kansas. The marriage was solemnized in Dodge City, Rev. C.M. Gray officiating.

The bride is the daughter of Mr. and Mrs. R.A. Slocum, of Dodge City, and is a young lady who is highly respected in that section of the state. For the past eighteen months she has filled the position of deputy county superintendent of Ford County and has a wide acquaintance over the county who recommend her very highly to our people.

George Gardner needs no introduction to our people — neither does he need any words of praise from a dinky editor like the writer — he is too well and favorably known over the county to require either. At the present election he ran far ahead on the ticket for sheriff and will take office the first of the year with the very best wishes of a wide circle of friends. At times like this we would like to swell up and say something nice about George, but everybody knows him so well and thinks so much of him that words seem empty and without meaning, and we shall only add that the young lady, Miss Margaret Slocum, got a fine gentleman for a husband, and we predict she will never have cause to regret her choice.

The happy couple will be at home to their friends in Oberlin in the next several days in a home prepared by the groom.

This Certifies that
G. W. Gardner
of Oberlin, Kansas
and
Margaret Slocum
of Dodge city, Kansas.
were by me united in
Holy Matrimony
at Dodge city, Kansas
According to the Ordinance of God
and the laws of Kansas
on the 8 day of December
in the Year of Our Lord 19 2 0
Mrs. C. M. Gray   C. M. Gray
Pastor M. E. Ch.

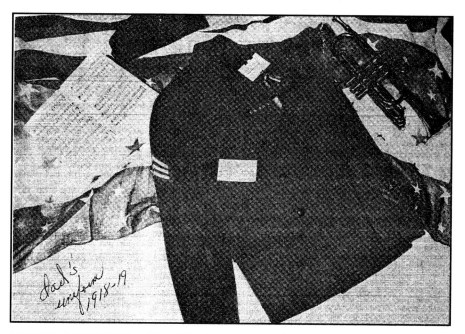

fad's uniform 1918-19

VETERANS DAY 1982 — World War I mementos remind Oberlin residents of the Thursday, Nov. 11 observance of Veterans Day to be held at 2:30 p.m. at the senior high gym at DCHS due to predicted inclement weather. Numerous business firms will be closed from 2:15 to 3:45 during the afternoon in order that persons may attend the Oberlin American Legion and Commercial Club sponsored every year. An open house and dinner will follow at the Legion. This year's observation of Veterans Day also coincides with the dedication of the Vietnam Veterans Memorial on Saturday in Washington, D.C.

(Obituary from the Oberlin Herald — 1965)

GEORGE GARDNER

Funeral services for George Gardner, 76, are pending with the Corcoran-Ready Funeral Home in charge of arrangements. He had been in ill health for several months and died late Monday night in the St. Luke's Hospital, Denver, where he had been a patient for a short time. Gardner, who was born northwest of Traer Nov. 14, 1888, was reared in that community. He entered the Army in 1917 at the beginning of WWI and was awarded the Distinguished Service Cross.

He and his wife, Margaret, moved to Oberlin in 1920 and purchased a farm about one mile southeast of Oberlin in 1924. In 1920, Gardner was elected as sheriff of Decatur County. He served four years as sheriff, four years as undersheriff, followed by 12 years as city marshal of Oberlin.

Survivors are his widow, Margaret; one daughter, Joyce Martin of Oberlin; one son, Kenneth of Venezuela, South America; one daughter-in-law, Mrs. Kenneth (Edith) Gardner of Redondo Beach, Calif.; five grandchildren and other relatives.

In Remembrance

God hath not promised
    Skies always blue,
Flower-strewn pathways
    All our lives through
God hath not promised
    Sun without rain,
Joy without sorrow,
    Peace without pain.

But God hath promised
    Strength for the day,
Rest for the labor,
    Light for the way.
Grace for the trials,
    Help from above,
Unfailing sympathy
    Undying love . . .

CORCORAN-READY

GEORGE W. GARDNER

BORN _____Nov. 14, 1888

PASSED AWAY:
April 19, 1965

SERVICES:
Corcoran-Ready Funeral Home
Saturday, April 24, 1965
2:00 p.m.

MINISTER:
Rev. H. G. Feldmann

SINGER:
Thomas McKay

ORGANIST:
Mrs. Lemoin Rush

SONGS:
"The Old Rugged Cross"
"Abide With Me"

CASKET BEARERS:

Walter Hatch	Edwin Robertson
Everett Smith	Leo Zodrow
Shirley Cochran	Jay Herzog

RESTING PLACE:
Oberlin Cemetery

GEORGE GARDNER
April 24, 1965

And this afternoon he was buried. How the event brings up a flood of memories to this 80-year-old farmer of Liberty Township.

I first knew George back in 1910 when I started going to dances at Traer, at first in a frame building that later burned. Then we danced in the cement block building we called Gardner's Hall. I'll come back to this later.

After I married in 1913, I didn't see much of George until the first world war draft. His number, 234, I think, was the first one drawn, and I heard about it that evening. There were three more names from Decatur County in that drawing: Leo Bendon, Glen B. Wookey and Ora L. Tilton. Tilton didn't respond to the call. He couldn't be found. But George, Leo and Glen left for camp in a big send-off.

The three men were sent to Fort Riley, I believe, to help prepare reception of the later draftees. And about the next time he came to my notice was when the report came that George and his squad captured a machine gun nest.

After he returned and ran for sheriff, the vote for him was about unanimous around here. I think he had the most difficult term of any sheriff that I know of. It was during prohibition days, and home brew makers were numerous.

But his most disagreeable job was when Bill McMullen insisted that he raid a gambling den north of town. George knew that one of his brothers was in the game, and it was in the home of a soldier friend. He could have warned them, but felt he had to fulfill his oath and went out and brought them in.

Another nasty job was when he had to arrest a boyhood friend at Traer for making booze. If I remember correctly, he also had to go to Traer and arrest his brother, Randolph. Another bad job was when a man wanted by the law in another state was sitting on the Oberlin depot platform. George received word the man was armed and dangerous. But he made the arrest.

When Tom McKay was reported missing, our county attorney refused to take any action, insisting it was one of Tom's jokes. But George, who was deputy then, was certain he'd been murdered and sent word over the party lines to search for the body.

Personally, I think he was one of the outstanding men of our county, but since he didn't get rich, he probably won't get the recognition he deserved.

Now to bring up some memories of those dances at Traer. The first one I went to early in 1909 was on the west side of the street (or road) in a building that later burned. I believe Hank Guinn was the fiddler, and it was a failure. Not enough women and girls for a square dance set — and ended in a squabble between Walt Castle and Sumner Payne. Nobody hurt. The next year we started dancing in the Gardner Building, sometimes on the lower floor and sometimes upstairs.

George's brother, John, had a hand in running the dances — about every other Saturday night. The fiddlers were Harry Rathbun, Eltie McCartney, Bill Hunter, and I think Anson Buzzell played some. An organ was used to second. Elmer Hunter and Annie Rathbun and I think John Gardner also seconded some. The callers were anybody we could coax. I remember one night the crowd was pretty scant and I was the only one who knew the figures. I did the best I could, but my voice was pretty weak for the job.

The front of the building was a barber shop. I think John Gardner did some of the barber work, also Frank Lipsey.

I think it was 25 cents apiece we men paid to dance for the evening. We quit at 12.

There weren't enough boys with team and buggy to bring the girls, so a number of the old folks came to bring them. I remember the Oliver McCartneys, the Floyd Harshmans, the August Wesches, the Hi Abbotts and a family named Clayton. Some of the couples that come to mind: Ben Bryan with Ethel Guinn; later Ethel came with Sumner Payne and Ben brought Birdie Harshman. Preston (Red) Elson with Mary Brown, John with Tracy Allacher; I brought Susie Leitner, later changed to Effie Mc. Ed Lipsye brought Tracy Rothmayer. Ed never danced but sat in the barber shop all evening. Hack Hayward and his sister Kate, Mahala Bryan (later Mrs. Roy Reed. Mrs. Joe Gragg (divorced) later Mrs. Archie Pryor. Fred Bisnett and sister Idea were always there. I think Newt Bryan and Maggie Patterson were going together then, but can't remember them dancing.

There was usually someone drunk, but I don't recall any real fighting except one night Eltie McCartney knocked Floyd Pierce across the sidewalk to quiet him.